Lost Souls

Inspiring Stories ʋ... basset Hounds

Kyla Duffy and Lowrey Mumford

Published by Happy Tails Books™, LLC

Happy Tails Books™ uses the power of storytelling to affect positive change in the lives of animals in need. The joy, hope, and (occasional) chaos these stories describe will make you laugh and cry as you em*bark* on a journey with these authors, who are guardians and/or fosters of rescued dogs. "Reading for Rescue" with Happy Tails Books not only brings further awareness to animal advocacy efforts and breed characteristics, but each sale also results in a financial contribution to dog rescue efforts.

Lost Souls: Found!™ Inspiring Stories About Basset Hounds by Kyla Duffy and Lowrey Mumford

Published by Happy Tails Books™, LLC   www.happytailsbooks.com

The publisher gratefully acknowledges the numerous Basset Hound rescue groups and their members, who generously granted permission to use their stories and photos.

Any brand names mentioned in this book are registered trademarks and the property of their owners. The author and publishing company make no claims to them.

Photo Credits (All Rights Reserved by Photographers):

> Front Cover & p84: Herbie, Susan Schmitz, www.adogslifephoto.com
> Back Cover Bottom Right: Emilee Fuss, www.emileefuss.com

Publishers Cataloging In Publication

Lost Souls: Found!™ Inspiring Stories About Basset Hounds/ [Compiled and edited by] Kyla Duffy and Lowrey Mumford.

p. ; cm.

ISBN: 978-0-9833126-2-8

1. Basset Hounds. 2. Dog rescue. 3. Dogs – Anecdotes. 4. Animal welfare – United States. 5. Human-animal relationships – Anecdotes. I. Duffy, Kyla. II. Mumford, Lowrey. III. Title.

SF426.5   2011

636.7536   2011905528

Happy Tails Books appreciates all of the contributors and rescue groups whose thought-provoking stories make this book come to life. We'd like to send a special thanks to:

Arizona Basset Hound Rescue

http://www.azbassetrescue.org/

Basset Rescue of the Old Dominion

http://www.brood-va.org/

Droopy Basset Hound Rescue

http://www.droopybassetrescue.com/

Golden Gate Basset Hound Rescue

http://ggbassetrescue.org/

Looziana Basset Rescue

http://www.petfinder.com/shelters/bayoubassets.html/

Ohio Basset Rescue

http://www.ohiobassetrescue.org/

Want more information about the dogs, authors, and rescues featured in this book? http://happytailsbooks.com

Table of Contents

Introduction: Answering the Call

It was very early during the morning of my second wedding anniversary, so I didn't answer the phone when it rang. I wanted to sleep in with my hubby. When I finally checked voicemail, it was the president of the rescue group for which I foster. The message simply said, "They found Bill. Call me."

I should have answered the call.

Bill was my two-year-old train wreck of a foster dog, whom I had only for an hour before he and another little girl I was fostering escaped from my yard. Well-socialized to people, the girl was found and returned immediately, but we were afraid Bill was gone for good. Terrified of people and completely unsocialized from spending his life in a cage at a puppy mill, Bill would try to get as far away from humans as possible. Three weeks passed, and I feared the coyotes had caught him, so the call that morning was shocking, to say the least. It was also ambiguous. Was he found alive? Dead? Where was he?

Joggers saw Bill in the woods about a quarter of a mile from my home, splayed out on a trail, trying to eat a carcass. They alerted animal control, who took him to our local humane society. His microchip was scanned, and he was subsequently reunited with our group.

Bill's future was uncertain. His three-week ordeal left him with a gash on his leg so deep that his muscle was exposed, and he was down to 13 pounds from 21, leaving his every bone protruding. He just sat, unresponsive, with no light in his eyes. His mood seemed similar to when I first got him, but physically he was much worse. Needless to say, I was overwhelmed with remorse but also driven to help him however I could, no matter what it would take.

For a month I took him to the vet every other day to get his bandages changed. For three months my husband and I hoped that he would start to move. Bill was so scared; he just sat in his bed and cowered. We carried him outside to potty, and then he would dart back to his bed. For a while we thought he would do best as a companion for a shut-in who did not have much activity in his or her home. However, after a time, Bill finally started to come around, and we decided that the best place for him was right here in our home.

With training (by my husband and me and by the dogs at the dog park), Bill started to gain confidence and understanding. He realized that we are here to love him and that he is supposed to play and enjoy life. We discovered that he loves hiking and romping through fields with other dogs, so we get him his "own" dog to foster as often as possible. Sometimes he's the big brother, and other times the fosters mentor him. Either way, it's always a great experience for us all.

Working with rescue groups (especially after Bill's fiasco) has given me much to reflect on. I cringe when I think about my best friend Bill's life at the puppy mill and lost in the woods. For a while, I felt completely helpless when considering the millions of other dogs also living without love, shelter, or proper medical care. Then, one day in my heart I "heard the call," and I wasn't going to miss it again. I realized that feeling helpless was not going to save lives. However, publishing books full of stories about wonderful adopted dogs and the positive impact they have had on their families, just might. This is how the *Lost Souls: FOUND!* book series was born.

If you read carefully, you'll surely laugh, cry, and learn from these amazing stories submitted by fosters and forever families, just as my co-editor Lowrey and I did when we edited them. I hope they will reinforce the belief that rescued dogs are exceptional dogs and are certainly worth the effort.

When you're finished reading, ask yourself if you've heard the call to support rescue. Volunteering, donating, or just sharing information are all valuable ways to help.

If you hear the call, don't let it go to voicemail. "Pick up the phone" and save a life.

 *Kyla Duffy, Editor-in-Chief*

Inspiring Stories About Basset Hounds

Counting Noses

When you have five dogs, you do a lot of counting noses. You do it when dispensing medicines, special meals and the like, especially with rescues. At any given meal, I could be heard muttering to myself, "One, two, three, four, and five," as I parceled out the goods. At the time, Harry, my Basset Hound, was suffering from glaucoma (the breed is susceptible to this painful eye condition), and he alone received 21 drops, pills, and salves each day in our attempt to save his eyesight.

On this particular day, I came rushing in the door later than planned to distribute everyone's evening meals. Truly, it wasn't that late, but they wear watches and *know* when it's feeding time. The horses were whinnying, and the pups were howling. So still in suit and heels, I doled out dinner (each of the five dogs ate something different, so I had to put each meal in the right spot). I uttered my traditional, "One, two, three, four, and five," even though there was a great deal of canine craziness rushing around me.

Alpha dog Winston, a rescue Basset/Beagle mix, decided to lecture me on my tardiness. Winston took his job as alpha dog seriously. He, too, counted noses, (canine, equine, and homo sapien), barking at offenders who snuck into the wrong eating area or attempted to grab a bite out of someone else's dinner. If I hadn't been late, I might have picked up sooner on the fact that my counting wasn't doing the trick. Somehow, on a recount I found, "One, two, three, four, five, and *six*."

Huh. I distinctly remember counting and thinking to myself, "I think we have an extra tail tonight," but then dismissing the notion. I *knew* I hadn't adopted anyone recently, and with my airtight security, escapees or break-ins were nonexistent.

I finished feeding the dogs, changed quickly to hand out medications, and then raced off to feed the horses. Once again, I had this nagging sense that my count for the night was off, but I kept telling myself, "Don't be silly. You have *five* dogs, not *six*."

Winston kept keening and dogging me as if I were missing an all-too-important message. If only I had listened better and sooner!

An hour later, after the horses were fed and the dogs medicated, Winston marched into my home office. He seemed quite indignant and howled up a storm. Okay, I thought. Something was bugging my elder statesman; something that seemed to be more important than just the fact that I was late. It was time to figure out what.

Winston and I went marching off to the doggie room, which is specially equipped with doggie beds, water, and even a lounging chair and ottoman for canine comfort, to determine the cause of the ruckus. "One, two, three, four, and five," I muttered before stopping dead in my tracks. There were six dogs in the room, and the newcomer was a dead ringer for Winston!

I looked back and forth between Winston and the visitor and was shocked at their mirror images. When I sat down to check out the new guy, I noticed he had no collar, but he was in very fine condition and as friendly as could be. My "kids" all acted as if this pup had been with them all their lives; their acceptance of him appeared instantaneous and complete. I was stunned. Where did he come from? More importantly, how did he get into my padlocked, completely fenced-in back yard?

I knew we had to find his family, so I immediately called the local humane society and posted information about him to various websites designed to help reunite dogs and their families. I also called the local emergency vet clinic, as harried and upset families often turn to vets to report their missing dogs.

After exhausting my resources to try and find his family, all I could do was wait. This dog, who I decided to name Bogart, seemed thrilled with his new digs, and his three brothers and two sisters seemed quite pleased to have a new member of the family. Even so, I just knew someone would call for him soon. Someone *had* to be looking for this beautiful dog. Although I live in an equestrian community, there are freeways to the east, major thoroughfares to the north, and large home developments to the south and west. His family had to be near. He couldn't have come from too far away.

Nearly a month passed since the mysterious arrival of Bogart—Number Six—and I still hadn't heard from anyone looking for him. I checked and rechecked the locks on the gates and walked all the fences, but I still could not figure out how he got into our back yard. None of my neighbors knew anything about him, and no one called. Bogart was just fine, but I was certain his family was missing him terribly, and that made me feel bad.

Then the call came! A gal from a neighborhood five miles away called to say a friend had been running and stumbled onto Bogart's now weather-beaten and mangled poster. Bogart would have had to cross two major intersections to get to my part of town from where this woman lived, with cars, trucks, and buses zipping by, so I held out little hope that she was his mom. Even so, I invited her to come see him and gave her directions to my home.

As usual, when I opened the front door to greet the woman, Winston marched out to check her out. The woman ran up the walk way upon seeing him and yelled, "Oh, it's Rusty!" I started to explain, but then she, too, realized Winston was not hers. Simultaneously, Bogart (really Rusty) heard his mom and began woofing up a storm before flying out the front door. Rusty and Mom had found each other!

We laughed excitedly over how much our two "boys" looked alike before Rusty headed home with his mom.

I was happy the two were reunited but still left to ponder how he got into our yard in the first place. A few days later, when a neighbor returned from a month-long trip, I had my answer. Upon seeing Winston and me picking up the mail, she waived and said, "Glad to see Winston with you."

I thought the comment was a bit odd, but at the moment it didn't register. Later that day, the neighbor called. She said that right before she left town, she found "Winston" pawing at the gate to get inside. She knew my pups are never allowed out without leashes and human escorts, so she grabbed my hidden key, opened the gate, and let "Winston" back in. She was just wondering how he had escaped. I laughed and told her the story, that the "Winston" she saw pawing to get in was actually "Rusty" the runaway, who had traversed over five miles to pay us a visit. She couldn't believe that Winston and Rusty could look so much alike!

The moral of this story is twofold. First, when counting tails, double check by counting noses! It's a surefire system to readily uncover any "visitors." And second, when your dog wants to tell you something, LISTEN!

 *Jeanette Harrison*

Saved by Serendipity

Bristow joined our family when we adopted him from the Arizona Basset Hound Rescue (AZBHR). I decided to join the rescue as a volunteer, and the following year I became the merchandise coordinator. When I signed up to volunteer, I had no idea what a gift AZBHR would be to my family.

Fast forward to February 7, seven years later, one of the saddest and scariest days of our lives. My husband, Rich, and I were on a camping trip with friends in Vekol Valley, Arizona, for the weekend. One of Rich's hobbies is powered paragliding, and the friends we went camping with were all pilots as well. We brought our RV, our two Basset Hounds, Bristow and Baxter, and our Chihuahua-mix, Lola, because we thought they would enjoy camping with us.

Some of the other campers were shooting guns and lighting firecrackers, and Bristow didn't have fun at all. He was very scared of the paraglider motor noise and all the noises from the other campers. He spent most of his time terrified in the backseat of the car.

On Sunday I left Bristow and Baxter in an X-pen (an enclosed exercise area) that we set up outside of our RV. I put out their kibble and walked over to the pilots' lounge for breakfast. I was only gone about 20 minutes, but in that time, someone started shooting targets, and I knew I had to get back to Bristow to comfort him. But by the time I returned to the X-pen, Bristow had escaped. We had no idea in which direction he had run. Luckily, Baxter was still there.

Rich and I started searching for Bristow with our friends, but we did not have much luck. It was too windy for anyone to take off and fly overhead to search, so we could only search on foot. Some of the guys found paw prints, and we tried to track them, but they only went so far before they disappeared. We walked and searched for him until it started getting dark.

At that point we had to make the difficult decision to travel 40 miles home and leave Bristow in the dark to fend for himself. We both cried on the way home in between making phone calls to family and friends. I contacted

AZBHR's president right away to see if she would send out a message to everyone to keep an eye out for any leads on a found Basset Hound matching Bristow's description.

We decided to not go to work the next day, so we could go back out to where we had lost Bristow and search again. My best friend, Rachael, came with me to search the ground, while Rich took to the air with our friend, Mo. That morning we walked the land while they scanned the sky for more than two hours. Rachael and I called for Bristow through a megaphone and shook his food bowl, hoping to see him come running. In the afternoon, four other pilots came out to search, along with a few other guys on foot. Unfortunately by nightfall, we still had no luck finding him. We spoke to some of people living in the area, and they all confirmed our worst fear: both coyotes and mountain lions inhabited the area. Our hope for finding Bristow was growing smaller by each hour.

The next day we headed into the town closest to the area where we had camped to put up signs and speak with local businesses. We put everyone we saw on the lookout for Bristow. When we came home we were restless because there were so many things that reminded us of Bristow, whether it was his resting his chin on my leg as we ate dinner or his snuggling against us in bed. It was such a painful time for both of us.

By Wednesday, we were so desperate to know if Bristow was still alive that we resorted to contacting a pet psychic. They always seem to have the right answers on TV, so how could it not work for us now? I just needed to know if we should give up and make peace with our loss or keep searching. The psychic told me that she believed his body had passed on, but his soul was still around to help us through this difficult time. She said that we should do something to honor Bristow's memory. That night Rich made a beautiful video with photos of Bristow. We posted it on Facebook to share with all of our friends. I still cry to this day when I watch it.

By Friday of that week, Bristow had been missing for five days. We decided to go back out to where we were camping and say our goodbyes. We walked the area again and had a moment of silence for him. We left there sad, but secretly we were both still hanging on to hope.

The following Monday was Presidents' Day, and I had the day off of work. I was busy running errands when I got a phone call from the vice president of the rescue. She said she had received a lead on a found Basset Hound who matched Bristow's description. I immediately called the woman and described Bristow's harness to her, and she said, "Yep, that's him!"

The couple lived nine miles from where we had been camping. She was a dog lover, too, with 14 Chihuahuas of her own at her house. She said that her husband had come in through their back door the night before and Bristow had just followed in behind him. Her husband hadn't even realized that Bristow was there! Bristow had immediately crawled onto their couch and howled at them. The couple had been kind enough to feed him and let him sleep on their bed for the night.

When we were finally reunited, Bristow had lost about six pounds and was very dehydrated, but he was happy to see us.

There were so many miracles in Bristow's return to our family. He survived for nine days in the desert; he found a family who loved dogs and took him in; the family who saved him didn't have access to the Internet, so it was through a friend that they contacted the rescue. Most often, when we receive a call on a found dog, the rescue refers it to the local shelter first. It was only because the shelters were closed for the holiday and my rescue friends knew Bristow's story that he was reunited with us. AZBHR saved Bristow's life twice.

I learned from this experience that you don't realize what an impact these beautiful animals have on your life until they aren't there anymore. After that experience, we'll never take our pets for granted; that's for sure!

 *Amy and Rich Rodriguez*

Just Ducky

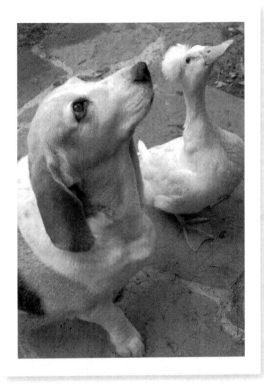

I ris is my blessing! Thank goodness she waited for me to find her. She had to spend over a year in the rescue system, due to her "special needs" after a life that was most likely spent in a puppy mill, a commercial breeding facility where breeding dogs receive little or no care at best, though abuse and neglect are most common. When I saw her picture on Basset Rescue of the Old Dominion's (BROOD) website and the story that went along with it, I was hooked.

It *only* took me five months to bring her home. When she arrived, she checked out every inch of her new yard and patio, and then went into the house for the total room nose-to-ground inspection. She found me and sat in front of me as if to say, "Okay, this is a place where I could be happy!"

Iris is the most compassionate, loving, companionable, entertaining dog we have ever had in over 40 years. Her tail never stops wagging as she waddles wherever she wants to go. She loves anyone she meets. She shares her home with three cats, two horses (more like at a close distance), numerous chickens, and most recently, an orphaned White Crested Peking duck, who has bonded with her and follows her everywhere! The duck has tried to get into Iris' dog bed to no avail.

Both my husband and I have had dogs our entire lives, but not one of them has affected us the way this lovely, nine-year-old beast has. Iris is my constant companion and my shadow, to the point of tripping me after being with us for three weeks. I broke my wrist and arm that time, but I don't blame her. She just wanted to be near!

Iris steals food when she can, she bawls at her convenience, she has a bed in every major room in the house, and she drools incessantly. But she loves me and mine, so hey, what more could I ask for? Her "special needs" are nothing compared to what she gives us, and I thank God every day that because of them, no one else wanted to deal with her.

How many people have seen a Basset Hound and a duck rushing after a ball, with the result of the duck getting bumped by the Basset's butt? Oh, to see them both in a wading pool together... Iris has brought us so much joy and laughter, and the stories of her antics just don't stop. We have had people stop their cars and bikes outside the gate and house to look at our dog and duck chasing each other. As I am writing this, the dog, the duck, and a cat are surrounding me, sleeping and waiting for snow to fall.

Iris must be an old soul reincarnated because we all feel we have known her forever. I don't know if that's because of her actions in her prior life or just because she is a Basset Hound, but I can't imagine a life without her.

 *Mary Biddle*

Hooter Mama

Joanie the Diva came into my life just a few days before Christmas. One look at her and I knew she was not going to leave my home. I would be a foster failure for sure (that's the endearing term we use in the "biz" when foster parents end up keeping their foster dogs). About two months prior to Joanie arriving at my house as my foster dog, my Beatrice (a.k.a. Queen Bea) had passed away very suddenly. I thought that fostering for Arizona Basset Hound Rescue (AZBHR) would be a great way to find a new Basset to join my family.

Joanie arrived at the rescue with her breeding mate, a 10-year-old male, but he quickly found his forever home. They had been used for breeding by a couple in Arizona, and when the couple had children, they no longer had time for the dogs. Joanie's nipples almost touched the ground, and you could easily tell she had been bred again and again. She came into heat while I was fostering her, but once her heat cycle was done, we spayed her, and finally I adopted her.

Joanie has a "you are lucky to have me" attitude, and I love her for it! She loves wet towels and playing in the laundry. If I throw a wet towel on her, she will roll around and frolic, making me smile and laugh. After I had her for a few weeks, she decided to play in my laundry and wound up with a bra on her head! That's when Joanie's new nickname became "Hooter Mama" due to her hanging "hooters" and the bra on her head.

This diva makes me laugh and loves to snuggle with Momma on the bed whenever she can. Even though she's an alpha female, we've had over 40 foster dogs come through our home over the years. She's learning to just deal with it, giving me "the diva look" and telling me how it is (she's a talker). I wouldn't have it any other way!

 *Kim A. Bruck*

Devotion beyond Diagnosis

Buddy first came into rescue as a young pup who had been dumped at a shelter. He went to live in a Basset Rescue of Old Dominion (BROOD) foster home, where he received lots of love and had plenty of room to run and play. When Buddy was one year old, he was adopted, but just before his second birthday, his new owners noticed he was not feeling well. They took Buddy to the vet and found out that he had Addison's disease (AD - an adrenal disorder causing myriad symptoms). Buddy spent some time at the vet hospital being treated and was finally ready to go home.

But Buddy couldn't go home.

Now that Buddy's family knew he had AD, they no longer wanted him. They ordered the vet to euthanize Buddy rather than send him home.

Thankfully, the vet refused and called BROOD instead. Since I was in charge of all the BROOD foster homes, I got the call that Buddy needed a place to live. I knew his chances of getting adopted weren't the best and that there was a chance he'd be with us forever.

We picked Buddy up on a hot August day, and I'll never forget the way he looked at me the first time I saw him. He wouldn't look at me straight on but only glanced at me out of the corner of his eye. It was apparent that he had no intention of getting friendly with anyone. He was fearful of what was to come, but I knew he was a gentle soul.

We took Buddy home to foster him, and within two weeks we were asking for adoption papers, so Buddy could stay with us forever. He was such a good addition to our home and our three other Basset Hounds, Molly, Maggie, and Watson, all welcomed him into their pack. Buddy was particularly close to Watson, whom we had also fostered for BROOD and then adopted. It was like they knew that they all had the fact they were once unwanted in common. They were best buds for the 8½ years they lived together.

Buddy did well and over the years became my heart dog. He loved me unconditionally and would bring me toys every time I came home. He was never more than a foot or two away from me, and he cried when I wasn't with him. He had many medical issues over the years, but we got through them. We made an early morning drive to the vet every third Saturday for his shot and checkup during his eight years with us. We made the 100-mile trek to Philadelphia when Buddy went lame and needed back surgery to walk again. We struggled through many unique situations, like when my silly boy ate everything in sight (pantyhose, boxes of Q-Tips, human medications, etc.). He was very sneaky, and hungry, apparently!

But through it all, my payback for the time and money we spent to give him the best life possible was the gift of being able to spend time with him. We loved each other totally. He died in his sleep a week and a day after Watson passed away. I was devastated to lose him but am so thankful that we had those years to share. I believe Buddy was a gift from God to me, and I was the lucky one for him to have found me.

 *Alisa Garbrick*

The Wonderful Mr. Rigby

Mr. Rigby is approximately nine years old. This tri-colored Basset Hound came into my life during a cold November five years ago. Back then I had just moved to the Washington, DC area and was not looking for a dog, but it was hard not to be drawn to Mr. Rigby when I saw him at an adoption show in front of a local pet store.

For a large Basset Hound, he was horribly malnourished. Stretched out on the sidewalk, his handsome head seemed unsupportable by an emaciated body whose every rib was visible. I spoke with his handler and learned that this poor boy, Rigby, had been found wandering in the woods in even worse shape. After several weeks of care, he still weighed in at only 38 pounds, which is 12 pounds less than what he carries today while looking trim.

I went into the pet store and bought him the biggest bone I could find. He picked himself up off the concrete, and within minutes he'd cracked the bone into pieces. I knew I had to leave soon, or I'd be taking this fella home.

One week later at the same time, I returned to the same pet store, and to my secret delight, Mr. Rigby was again in attendance, slightly heavier and more animated. I bought him another bone and watched him make short work of it. But once again, I left without taking the plunge.

Another week lapsed, and I was drawn back to yet another adoption show. As you may have guessed, Rigby was there. But there was another twist to his story. He had spent a few days of the last week in a new home, only to be returned for stealing food off a kitchen counter. I was amazed that a Basset Hound could pull off such a feat, surprised that his new family would have rejected him for it, and secretly relieved that I had not missed my chance to rescue Rigby. I filled out the paperwork right then and there. In keeping with his proud appearance, I added the "Mr." to his name, and thus commenced my life with Mr. Rigby.

No doubt, nearly everyone who has a dog loves to gush about how wonderful his or her particular pet is. Forgive me my bias, but Mr. Rigby is the most wonderful dog in the world (aside from his brother, a 10-year-old rescued Cocker Spaniel named Duke). He is wonderfully willful, for instance, demanding 10-minute belly rubs whenever he wakes from his 12-hour naps. He's wonderfully stubborn, like when he routinely digs in his heels while we're attempting to cross busy thoroughfares. He is wonderfully self-absorbed, staring for hours at nothing, or at least nothing that I or even Duke find worthy of a moment's notice. And he's wonderfully assertive. He barks out his requests to be carried downstairs (for the last year arthritis has curtailed his ability to descend on his own but hasn't weakened his conviction that the mattress in the second-floor bedroom is the most comfortable spot in the house for dozing). But most of all, he is wonderfully loved by just about everyone (human and canine) who crosses his path.

On our many walks, slowed to an aging Basset Hound's pace while Duke strains for more speed, nearly every passerby smiles after they've gazed down at Mr. Rigby in his contentment. That's his gift to us: his gentle nature and the smiles it evokes. It is wonderful indeed.

 *David Posner*

Hometown Harley

T his past February I received an email from Arizona Basset Hound Rescue (AZBHR) about a hoarder in Douglas, Arizona, from whom Douglas Animal Control had confiscated eight Basset Hounds. They brought the dogs up to Benson, where they were then transported to Tucson. They all were in very good condition and very friendly: six puppies along with their mom and dad.

This email was especially interesting to me because my husband is from Douglas, and you don't hear much about it. I already had two dogs and wasn't sure if I was ready to add another dog to my family. I was still mourning the loss of my Basset Hound, Lucy. I thought my nine-year-old Basset Hound, Ricky, might commit doggy suicide if I brought another dog in so soon. So in light of that, and since the dogs wouldn't be ready to be adopted out for awhile because they needed to be neutered, my husband and I kind of dropped the idea. Well, I think *he* dropped it, but I kept it in the back of my mind.

Leave it to the rescue to keep sending out updated pictures of the puppies. I had to forward the pictures to my husband, and he finally said, "Okay, let's go see them."

Now, when my husband said that, what he really meant was, "Okay, which one of them are we going to be adopting?"

And, of course, upon hearing that, I was already thinking of names, not even knowing which one we would be adopting or whether it would be a male or female.

We arrived at the foster home, and once we held each one, we wanted them all! It was a hard decision, but one puppy stood out, the smallest of the bunch. Her name was Hannah, and she was adorable. My husband picked her up first, and it was love at first sight. I already knew which dog we were adopting at that point. Hannah would be the third addition to our family.

A couple of weeks before we were to adopt Hannah, we received an email from the foster momma telling us that Hannah, now Harley in our minds, had a bad reaction to her parvo shot. Her hind leg swelled and the bubble that appeared from the shot burst. She had to be rushed to the vet so he could drain it and stitch it up.

We were scared, but she got through it fine. Harley is doing well now, although she has a scar to remind us of it. These days she can have regular shots with no problems.

Harley has been a great addition to our family, even though my 10-year-old, Ricky, might say otherwise. We love her and thank AZBHR for bringing us our puppy from Douglas, the small town where my husband grew up.

 *Stacey and Troy Lent*

Journey of Redemption

The tale of Josie and Amaryllis is a journey of redemption. It begins with a less-than-perfect, under-loved Basset named Josie and the mixture of sadness and guilt we experienced upon her passing. The story continues with Amaryllis, a stray dog adopted through rescue, and how she and her new people, who were determined not to repeat their old mistakes, worked hard together so that this time their Basset could become a beloved member of the family.

My husband and I had always had a dog or two or three, and one of them was always a Basset Hound. We raised Josie from a just-weaned pup who was all ears, belly, and paws. She was absolutely adorable, and she needed to be since she was also one of the most stubborn individuals of a very stubborn breed!

Over the years, as we became busy with work, children, and a family illness, she and our other two dogs, a rescued Sheltie and an American Eskimo, gradually started getting less of our time. We often had to hope it was enough that they had each other. Josie was not mistreated, starved, or left out in the cold, but between our reactions to the less-than-loveable results of her stubbornness and our busy schedule, she just never seemed to get enough good attention.

As they grew old together and became ill, we had to put our dogs down, one by one. Josie was the last of the three when at 14 she developed a stomach problem, which made it progressively harder for her to eat. When, in her infirmity, we began to give her more attention, we felt guilty that we had neither spent enough time with her earlier nor loved her as much as we should have. She had deserved better. We decided we never would, and possibly never should, have another dog. Certainly never another Basset Hound!

Our family and friends thought differently. A couple who had three rescued Basset Hounds waited almost a year after Josie's death before they emailed us about some young females who were up for adoption in our area. We didn't look at the email. We didn't want or think we deserved another dog. But we also didn't delete it.

Over time our viewpoint began to soften. We missed the good times with our dogs. But there also had been those bad behaviors, which we had not known how to fix, and which had been so disruptive that we simply couldn't tolerate them in our house again.

But what if we could do something different with a new dog? The unwanted behaviors could be avoided. If we learned more about dog behavior and consistently provided enough time, patience, and loving discipline, we thought we could watch for and correct bad behaviors early. We could influence a new dog to become well-behaved. (What a concept!)

Not long after Josie died, our home situation changed in a way that solved our time problem. I retired because of illness and was home alone all day. There would be plenty of hours to play with a new Basset Hound companion and have a schedule that would include walks, as weather and health permitted.

We knew it would help to formally train a new dog. Since we didn't know how to do that, we found a good obedience school. We decided on individual classes, since we would be adopting an adult dog who might have any number of special problems. We further resolved to be unfailingly patient and loving during the process; after all, this would be a rescued dog, and she might have been abused.

Then we found our Amaryllis. We had narrowed the choice down to two seemingly similar Bassets and then picked her because of her name. Don't you just love the irony of a dainty flower name for a big, sturdy Basset Hound girl? She was a young stray, a recent mother who had heartworm when she was found. And she was a sweetheart with big brown eyes filled with devotion.

During the first month, Amaryllis stood behind my feet, broadside, in the kitchen, so I tripped over her constantly. She interrupted our sleep as she roamed the house, coming to our bed often in the night for belly rubs and pats of reassurance. She bolted out the door between our legs twice in the direction of the main road, and we had to chase her in the car for a long time before we could catch her. I can't deny that for the first month or so there were times when we wondered what insanity had possessed us!

Sometimes, when it seemed Amaryllis might never settle in, I would take a deep breath and whisper, "This is for what I didn't do for you, Josie," and we'd just keep trying. Obedience training helped us learn how to listen to each other, respect each other, and play together. It also taught Ammy something she surprisingly didn't know: how to play with other dogs. Doggie school taught us both so very much more than just a few commands, and I would recommend it to anyone who has not gone through it and who wants to have a better relationship with their pet.

It has been five months since Ammy joined our family. Obedience school is over, and she did great for a Basset Hound, finishing tied for fourth place in a testing group of five! We have love, mutual respect, a schedule, and a deep understanding. She generally waits to be invited now before coming out a door. Once, when she did run off, she actually stopped and came when I called her. She is by my side all day. She still stands behind me in the kitchen, but I don't trip now because I know she's there. She loves walks, car rides, people, and other dogs. She is extremely gentle, but I know she'd protect me if the need arose.

Ammy has unique talents that I might never have noticed if we weren't such constant companions. She intentionally tosses one ear over her eyes if it's too bright when she wants to sleep. She howls soprano, usually on pitch, when I practice voice. She sorts her toys by size and type: Large bones in one spot, small bones in another, and furry squeaky toys in yet another. Sometimes she lines her toys up, perfectly spaced, across the living room carpet, or she uses them to make geometric figures (squares and triangles). Who'd have thought? My husband found one such display, and it took some convincing that I hadn't done it to fool him!

We learned that it takes open hearts, mutual respect, and the educated hard work of us all to make a happy family that includes our dog. As Ammy might say, good things happen when you're willing to put your nose to the ground and run the distance!

So here's to you, Amaryllis, a Basset Hound who has in a very short time earned those four words of highest canine praise: "You're a Good Dog!" And here's to you, too, Josie, for showing us the way.

 *Cynthia R. Smith*

Senior Sentiment

I remember the first day I met my Nelly Belle as if it were just yesterday. She was a little senior Basset, whom many people had just passed by. I thought of all the excuses they probably made: She needs too much medical care; she smells bad; she is fearful; she is too old (the worst they could say!). What they didn't see was that in those vacant-looking eyes, there was a tiny, almost-hidden spark that just needed a little help igniting. I knew within moments that I could not leave her behind. This tiny, red-and-white basset was coming home to live out the rest of her senior years, no matter how long that would be.

Yes, there were many challenges to overcome, like getting her to just come in the front door. Everyday noises such as the clinking from putting a glass down would send her scurrying for her safe spot under the bed, but I would not give up on her as others had. Together we faced and overcame her fears. All it took was time, patience, and most of all, love. The first time she gave me her sweet, upturned belly for a rub I knew that we had crossed a milestone. Tears of pure elation streaked my face when months later I received my first kiss from my girl.

My sweet Nelly Belle, who had never lived in a house, who was thrown away because she was "too old," has blossomed into an amazing senior am-Basset-dor. Nelly Belle has shown me that loving a senior is one of the purest loves you will ever find. Many have told me what a lucky girl she is, but I know I am the one who is truly blessed.

 *Karen Metcalf*

The Bashful Basset

Baxter began his life as a puppy mill dog, spending about two years in some pretty bad conditions. Arizona Basset Hound Rescue (AZBHR) saved Baxter and a few other dogs about 5½ years ago. Shortly after that we adopted him, and that's where his story really begins.

Unfortunately, Bax never had a chance to know what being a puppy was all about. His only human contact must have been painful because he spent the first month cowering in the corner of our yard. Each night we would have to surround him in order to bring him inside for bed. He did seem to like his daily walks, but getting a leash on him was a chore.

A lot changed when we adopted a second Basset Hound, Gallagher, the following April. Gallagher came through AZBHR as well, but since he was raised in a private home, he loved everyone and figured everyone would automatically love him. He immediately took Bax under his paw, so to speak, and showed him that it could be fun to be a dog with belly rubs, treats, and long walks.

Despite Baxter's progress, there have understandably been a few setbacks. One summer the family—Dad, Mom, and two Basset Hounds—set off cross country for a visit with relatives in our fifth wheel. Between Illinois and Minnesota we stayed in a lovely RV Park that was surrounded by woods, about a half mile from the Mississippi River. One afternoon we headed down the steps of the RV with both dogs, ready to put their leashes on and go for a walk, when Bax just kept walking. We called him, and it was as if he were deaf and blind. He just kept walking. There began the worst 12 days of our lives.

The entire RV Park searched for him, and the neighbors on nearby farms came out with their dogs, to no avail. We knew he was still around because he was spotted in the woods near the campground, but he would not come out. Two little girls were camping with their families and had set up a separate pup tent for their own camping experience. They said they could hear his tags jingling during the middle of the night, and they made it their quest to catch him. The city animal shelter lent us a cage, and the girls baited it with hot dogs. On the second night around 2 a.m., the girls heard his jingling. It was Bax. When he got into the cage, the girls closed the door, and the rest is history. Needless to say, both girls received a very generous reward from us.

Twelve days in the Minnesota woods and Baxter was no worse for wear. A trip to the local vet showed that he'd lost a few pounds but was in good health. When he was returned to us, you would have thought nothing had happened. From that day forward, Baxter never walked out of our home unless he had his leash on.

Our latest "episode" with our very special boy happened just a little over a month ago. We got up at 6:30 a.m., and when we opened the door to let the dogs out, Baxter just lay in his bed. He could not stand; his back legs could not support him. Our veterinarian in Yuma said to bring him right in, and we left him there for tests. The call came about noon. Baxter had ruptured at least one disc and would need the help of a specialist if he was going to have any chance. We made an appointment for him at the Neurological Center in Phoenix, 160 miles from our home! We got there at three in the afternoon, and by the evening CT scans and MRIs had shown the doctors that Baxter had ruptured not one but two discs. Immediate surgery was necessary. Baxter got out of surgery at 10 p.m., and the doctor said she thought he might have a chance since his spinal cord looked good. He came home with us the following Monday, and then we began the long road to recovery.

Since "Mom" had to leave town the following week for radiation treatments due to breast cancer, "Dad" was the nurse on duty. He built a box with sides, so Baxter couldn't move around and pull his catheter out. Then he put the box on a furniture dolly, so he could move it in and out of the house. Following the removal of the catheter, there were lots of clean ups and lots of baths and still more laundry. We drew up a calendar with the times for all his medications. At one point he was taking eight pills a day. Bodily functions became a cause for celebration, resulting in a call to Mom to report in.

Baxter is nothing if not determined. He has since regained his ability to stand alone and walk, although a bit unsteadily, and has developed a funny little "bunny hop" when he wants to get somewhere in a hurry. There are still times when he tires and just drags himself around, but he does manage to get where he wants to go. His daily walks have resumed with the aid of a wonderful tool called the Bottoms Up Leash, which helps support his weak back legs and allows freedom of movement. It's been five weeks since his surgery, and we are confident that he'll make a full recovery.

Baxter will probably always be shy of strangers and flinch at loud noises and quick movements, but he's come a long way in the four years we've been lucky enough to be his family. All of his problems and his recoveries have kept us busy, and we like to think of him as the most-loved Basset Hound west of the Mississippi.

 *Marge Robison*

We Go Together

Beatrice the Basset Hound adopted me the moment I met her at her foster home in Milwaukee, Wisconsin. After adopting Beatrice, a.k.a. Queen Bea, from Basset Buddies Rescue in Wisconsin, I accepted a job offer with a company in Phoenix, Arizona. That meant Beatrice and I would be moving.

Beatrice had been with me about six months when we loaded up the car to move to Phoenix. My mom, Grandma Bruck, Beatrice the Basset, and I headed on the road from South Milwaukee to Phoenix with a few stops planned along the way. Our first sleepover was at my friends' house in St.

Louis, Missouri. The Bartlows' cat didn't mind Beatrice, but it seems Beatrice was a bit afraid of the cat, so she just kept her distance.

Beatrice was a great passenger and never complained as we traveled for many hours each day. We'd stop to give her some walking time, water, and a few treats, of course. We made the trip in four days, staying in three cities along the way. We made stops to do some shopping, taste some wine, and buy dog treats. Beatrice was the best, never complaining in a Hound kind of way at all.

We arrived in Phoenix and moved into our new apartment on a 100-degree day in June. Beatrice adjusted well to the move, new apartment, and most of all, the weather. She then moved with me to our new home before passing away at the age of 12, just 2½ years after arriving in Phoenix.

I've been a volunteer for the Arizona Basset Hound Rescue for many years, and Beatrice is the reason I help the Basset Hounds, the breed I love. It amazes me how many people turn their dogs into rescue groups because they are moving. I'll never understand how someone can give away their dog when they have to move. There is no way I'd ever give up one of my Basset Hounds. There are so many pet-friendly hotels, apartments, and homes you can rent along the way to your destination. A move can be stressful for you, but imagine what your pet is thinking. "Why are you leaving me? What did I do wrong? I'm sorry, I promise...."

Not my Hounds. Where I go, they'll always go, too.

 *Kim A. Bruck*

We made a long distance move by car, from Pennsylvania to Louisiana, along with our two dogs: Mabel, our 14-year-old Basset Hound and Jingle, our 11-year-old Basset/Beagle mix. Mabel was doing well despite chronic renal failure, but three months after our move, she began to fail. We lost her a month later.

Needless to say, Jingle was very lonely after Mabel's passing. She would spend her days lying in the yard, staring off, waiting for Mabel to return. It broke our hearts to see her so sad. We knew we had to find her a new friend, so we contacted Looziana Basset Rescue (LBR).

After hearing about our situation, Leslie, the rescue's president, suggested Louise. She thought this three-year-old Basset Hound, who had been picked up as a stray, would be a good fit for our family.

Leslie was so right! Louise was, and is, perfect for us. Despite her previous sad times, she is a wonderfully outgoing, happy-go-lucky girl, who absolutely lives for belly rubs! She will immediately stop, drop, and roll for anyone, allowing strangers to rub that belly for as long as their hands can hold out.

Louise is a friend to all, except squirrels, which she taunts daily. Of course, they taunt her just as much in return.

We've nicknamed her Easy Ouisi because she fit into our family so fast and, well, so easily! We love her with all of our hearts and are so grateful to LBR for bringing this lovable, loving, sweet, funny girl into our lives.

 *Debbie Berthelot*

Biscuit Power

When I lost my Basset Hound, Bud, after 14 years, my heart and my world were shattered. He had been there for me through everything. He watched my twin daughters grow up and listened to me complain through their teenage years. He supported me through our move from Canada to Alabama. He was a warm companion at my side through chemotherapy, and he was never confused by my erratic behavior through menopause. My rock, my go-to-guy, was gone. I was a mess.

Though I had never written a poem before, I felt compelled to put the pain of my loss into words:

"The Spot"

There's a spot on my floor that I cannot erase.
There's a spot on my couch, that's a glaring bare space.
There's a spot by my bed, like a hole in the floor.
There's a spot in the kitchen, by the pantry room door.
There's a spot by the table, where we ate our meals.
There's a spot in my heart that will never heal.
These spots can't be cleaned, can't be scrubbed or replaced.
They're a painful reminder that I now have to face.
All of these spots were made by one friend.
He was soft; he was gentle; he was true 'til the end.
I will miss him forever; I just hope that he's found
A spot where he's happy, 'til I come back around.

Everything had changed. Every room was empty. We had two other dogs, whom I loved very much, but the house was still empty. I missed my old Hound.

I found comfort in looking at video clips and pictures of Basset Hounds. I would sit at my computer for hours, crying and laughing at Youtube videos. I also looked at a variety of breeders' sites. I smiled as I looked at the adorable puppies, but I knew it was not a puppy I wanted. I longed for the comforting snores of my old senior Basset, Bud.

We had never adopted before, but I found myself captivated by all of the beautiful souls on Petfinder.com. There were more than 2,000 available Basset Hounds. Through my tears I looked at Hound after Hound, waiting for a sign.

Suddenly, there she was! Her resemblance to my Buddy was almost spooky. Her kennel name was Dharma, and she had been rescued by The Ohio Basset Rescue (OBR) after being discarded by a breeder. I called her foster mom, Barb, to learn more. She was in rough shape when OBR got her. Many of her teeth had rotted due to lack of calcium during her breeding days. The veterinarian had to remove 18 teeth. They don't know how long she had been on her own, but it took several baths just to determine the color of her fur. OBR spent a great deal of time, energy, money, and, of course, love to prepare Dharma for adoption. But there she was, ready for her new home.

The more Barb told me about her, the more I knew she was meant to be mine. She said Dharma was afraid of storms and fireworks, she was a messy drinker, and she shed like a bear. She was always hungry, and if Barb didn't feed her in a timely manner, she would find a way of feeding herself, including opening Barb's fridge. She was perfect! There was just one *big* problem. Our family lives in Alabama, and Dharma was in Ohio. OBR takes adoption very seriously, as they should, and they were not eager for out-of-state adoptions.

I would not take no for an answer. I persisted, and finally, after many reference checks with my vets and neighbors, we were approved.

We drove 800 miles to pick up our girl. As we got closer, I started to feel anxious. What if she was not what I expected her to be? What if she did not like us?

Finally we arrived. We knocked on the door, and Barb answered, inviting us into the living room. Dharma had been with Barb for six months, and Barb loved her very much, so I am sure that she, too, was filled with mixed emotions. After chatting for a few moments, Barb brought Dharma into the room. She was beautiful. Much skinnier than our big boy, Bud. She was shy at first,nervously barking at us, but eventually she came into the room and sat at Barb's feet. We waited a while until she felt a bit more at ease, and then I brought out the big artillery: a biscuit. Oh, I have been a Basset Hound parent for 25 years, and I knew the power of the biscuit. It worked, and before long she was leaning up against us. We felt good, and I think Barb did, too.

We packed up Dharma's leash, collar, some snacks, and her stuffed doggy, and we were on our way. She jumped in the back seat without a second thought and was a perfect passenger all the way home.

When we arrived home after our long journey, Dharma pranced through the front door and made our home her own immediately. Our young Basset girl, Mona, rushed to the door thinking Dharma was her Bud. She had known Bud her whole life and had been mourning his loss. She got within about two feet and slammed on the brakes, realizing the dog at the door was someone else. Nevertheless, they bonded almost immediately.

After getting to know Dharma, we renamed her Bunny. She is our Honey Bunny.

Bunny enjoys the southern life: long walks amongst the trees, wading into the streams, and baking her belly in the sun. She has added some "curves" to her once slimmer body, but she is healthy and happy and loved.

Bunny did what I thought could never be done. She filled the hole in my heart. Today is her 11th birthday. As I write, she sits at my side, snoring in the sun. A hint of "eau de basset" fills the air. It is heaven. We often tell her that she hit the Basset lottery when we adopted her, but we really know that it is us who have won.

This wonderful experience of adoption has motivated me. I now volunteer for one of our local animal shelters, Animal Rescue Foundation (ARF) of Mobile. I have adopted two more wonderful furkids from the ARFanage. There really is nothing more fulfilling than saving a furry soul and likewise being saved.

 *Cindy Ferguson*

Once is Enough

leanor, a Basset Hound, came into my life when I helped transport her to a vet in Huntley, Illinois. She touched my heart so much within those initial 24 hours my husband and I decided to foster her. After a week at the vet for medical attention, I went back to pick her up.

Imagine my distress when I arrived at the vet's office to find out that she had escaped that morning! Eleanor was a rescue dog from another state. No one knew much about her other than that she was running scared and would not go near any human being! BREW Midwest volunteers, Basset Buddies Rescue volunteers, and the community of Huntley all got involved in the quest of bringing Eleanor to safety.

We passed out 2,000 flyers and posted signs on street corners. The word went out on the Internet, and we consulted with lost dog professionals from Boston to Arizona. We tracked local sightings on a map, and we set up a humane trap with a feeding station where she had been recently seen. It was manned at all hours of the day and night; we needed to find her! One BREW Midwest volunteer, Wayne, even camped out in his van for numerous nights just for a chance to catch a glimpse of our girl.

After 29 agonizing days, Eleanor was finally captured in the humane trap at 2 a.m. Wayne had been camping out that night and saw the whole event unfold. It was such a relief, and I got chills when he called to say, "I got her."

I drove to the trap site in shock and kept hoping that this wasn't a dream. When I pulled in and saw Eleanor in the trap, I was able to breathe a sigh of relief. I carried her to the car with *two* leashes on her! This girl wasn't going to get away again.

After fostering Eleanor for a little over 24 hours, my husband and I signed the adoption papers. Eleanor is now Ellie; after all, a new beginning deserves a new name. Ellie joins our rescued family of Elroy (a Beagle/Basset Hound or "Bagel" mix), Ricky and Gracie (Beagles), Tippy (Ellie's best bud, a Chihuahua puppy mill survivor), Bert and Ernie (Lovebirds), Bob (Senegal parrot), and Elvis, whom we just added to our mix. My husband lovingly calls Elvis a "Clydeshound" because of his size, but he's really an 11-year-old, 105-pound Bloodhound/Coonhound mix. We are all as happy as can be!

 *Susan Taney*

He Had Me at "Woof"

During the third week of February, I walked into our local Feeder's Supply Store to purchase a new collar for our then five-year-old Basset Hound, Molly. As I was looking at the selection of collars, I heard, "Woof!" from the far back corner of the large store, some 75 feet away. Instantly recognizing it as a Basset Hound's voice, I walked back toward the "Woof!" to say hello.

There he was sitting in a cage with a $134 price tag on him. He looked up at me through the cage and again said a softer, "Woof!" raising his right front paw as if to say, "Howdy!"

He must have looked across that long store aisle and seen "SUCKER" written all over me.

Feeder's Supply allows the local humane society to advertise their animals at the store, and he was part of the display. I reached through the cage and was greeted by a big, soft, pink tongue eagerly licking my hand. I spoke with him for a while and then asked the attendant about him and why this beautiful purebred animal was only $134. The lady told me his name was Roscoe and that he was five years old. She said he was so reasonably priced because he had been with them for a long time. Roscoe had been rescued in a neighboring county and had been with the humane society since the third day of January. He was housetrained and seemed to do well with people and smaller dogs. He had arrived with the name Roscoe and appeared to identify well with it.

The lady told me he would be a "hard adoption" because of his age and size. Roscoe is a *big* boy. He weighs 73 pounds, which is all muscle, ears, and pink tongue. The lady said older folks didn't want him because he was so strong, and families with little kids were looking for Basset Hound puppies. I could visualize Roscoe sitting in that cage for a long time.

I said goodbye to Roscoe and told the lady I would talk with my wife about him and get back with the humane society folks later that day, but if some good family walked in and would be willing to take him and care for him, to let them have him. We had never before adopted a mature dog, but when I called my wife at her office to discuss Roscoe, she immediately said to go back and get him! I told her, "No, we have Molly to think about, and I'd really rather take Molly to meet Roscoe and see how they interact before doing something like that."

When my wife got home from work, together we took Molly to visit with Roscoe in the store's warehouse-like storage room. Molly and Roscoe were buddies from the start, running and chasing and playing all over that room, dodging around pallets of dog food and supplies. Store employees were coming back there to watch those two Basset Hounds run and bark and play. It was a done deal, and Roscoe came home with us.

Roscoe has the curiosity of a cat, and immediately upon entering his new home, this big and powerful animal ran around the house like a little kid on Christmas morning to see it all at once, before it got away from him. As he ran, he excitedly barked, and his tail wagged fast and furiously. Molly ran right at his side, as if she was taking him on a tour of the place. The boy was excited!

That evening, and every evening for the first week he was here, as I sat in my favorite chair reading or watching TV, Roscoe came to me and crawled his massive body up into my lap to lie across my chest, with his head on my right shoulder. He gently nuzzled my ear and drifted off to a pre-bedtime nap. It was almost as if he knew he was home and safe, and he was thanking me for adopting him.

It has now been over a year since we brought Roscoe home. All of us, including Molly, love the big lug to death. Roscoe was housetrained as promised, but his manners were a little rough. He is still learning, and at times he still does not know his own strength and size. He thinks he is still a puppy. We do not know anything about Roscoe's past, but he seems to really like little kids and small dogs, immediately wanting them to play chase with him. We have reason to believe he may have been attacked by a Pit Bull or Pit Bull-mix in his past, since any time he sees an animal like this, he turns from "Jekyll" into "Hyde." This strong, lovable lug, who is far from being an alpha dog, becomes aggressive and tries to get to the animal. This saddens me to think of what his life may have been like before us.

Roscoe loves walks and car rides. In his former life, he somehow came to know the McDonald's Golden Arches sign, and if he sees one out the car window, he goes bananas, almost pleading with us to pull in there. Also, Roscoe has road rage. As long as the car is moving, he's content to be looking around with what almost seems like a Basset smile on his mug. But if we get caught by a traffic light, he loses it! He begins with small, plaintive whines, and by the time a long-holding light has turned green, he has gone bonkers in the back seat: barking, blowing slobbers, and jumping up and down! I'm sure neighboring vehicle occupants think I have a rabid animal in my back seat. As soon as we are able to drive on, he's his old self again.

I look forward to what I hope will be a *long* life with both my Basset buddies!

 *Roy Nall*

Disaster Turned Dream Dog

Six years ago we started volunteering for Droopy Basset Rescue. Our first foster dog was Gretta, an eight-year-old princess who was obviously used to running the house. She soon took over our home, dominating our other dogs and us. After she attacked my husband and sent one of our dogs to the vet for bite wounds, we knew we had to do something. We were not used to aggressive dogs, and we needed help!

We had been watching *The Dog Whisperer* television show for a couple of years, and upon reading his first book and consulting a local trainer, we put his techniques to work. The process was slow, as we were still learning, but with time and patience we learned how to help Gretta build confidence and become a comfortable member of our pack.

We ended up adopting Gretta, and we often kid her that this was her reward for turning over a new leaf. But it was really Mark and I who reaped the rewards of turning a difficult dog into a loving one.

We lost Gretta to cancer last year, but she will never be forgotten. She made it possible for us to continue fostering both well-behaved dogs and not-so-perfect dogs. I once heard the saying, "You never get the dog you want, but you get the dog you need."

We needed Gretta at least as much as she needed us, and we will forever be grateful for what she taught us. Thank you, Gretta!

 *Diane Burns*

From Fears to Family

Eight in the morning: All four hounds are fed and down for the morning nap. Now it's my time to read the daily e-mail from BROOD (Basset Rescue of the Old Dominion) called *The Rambler*. I sit down with my coffee, open it up, and there it is: A call for fosters; the kennel is closing for awhile.

Without hesitation, I e-mail the group and tell them, "Yes, we will take one." I hit the send button and then called Phil at work .I slowly pose the question, "Do you think we could take in another dog to foster?"

Without a real answer, he asks, "When do we pick him up?"

Later that evening a reply comes back saying they are glad but warning us of the dog's state of mind. Turns out this seven-year-old Basset Hound has not been socialized and is more than shy. He needs a lot of support.

I write back to say we'll give it a try, and our weekend plans are set. We're getting a new foster dog!

Saturday comes fast. We eat a light breakfast, gather up the gang—Maggie, CeCe, Willie, and Poppie—and head down the road. Forty-five minutes later we pull up to the entrance of the kennel, and before the car completely stops, I'm opening the door, grabbing the lead, and heading out. As I open the front door of the kennel, I see the kennel caretaker sitting on the floor, tightly holding a beautiful, tiny Basset Hound, who is shaking harder than any I have ever seen. He's trying to hide his head under her arm.

I go over to them and reach out to touch him, but he is terrified and now pushing his head further between her back and the wall, madly trying to escape from me. I take a step back and begin to tear up. It takes a moment to compose my thoughts, but then I ask about his temperament. I'm told that he's scared of people and has been observed fence fighting. He doesn't seem to get along with other dogs. I excuse myself to go grab Phil and confess to him privately that I don't think I have enough experience to handle this dog along with our four.

When Phil gets inside, he tries to get near this dog, Pannie. But from Pannie's reaction, you would think that Phil is a monster! The poor dog is absolutely out of his mind with fear.

Phil goes back to the car, and I tell the lady that I am sorry, but I cannot take him home. I run to the car, and once inside

I begin to cry and cry. I cry all the way home. After settling in for the evening, I e-mail the group and let them know my decision. They say they understand but remind me that he is one of the last to find a foster because of his behavior.

As the evening progresses, all Phil and I can do is talk of the little Basset Hound. On Sunday we decide we have to give him a try because dogs like Pannie are why we are involved with rescue. We have to help the ones who have slim chances.

Monday comes. Phil decides to go get Pannie after work. Of course, it starts snowing and then snowing *hard* around noon. At 3 p.m. I see sleet. I called Phil and tell him that Pannie can wait for one more day, but he firmly says, "No. He is not spending one more day at the kennel. He needs us. I will be fine."

Phil calls me on his cell as he pulls into the yard with Pannie, and I begin gathering the hounds to meet the new guy. Phil holds Pannie, while I take each dog to meet him, and then we muzzle them all and let them loose in the back yard. The poor little guy just wants to find a place to hide, but at least nobody bites anybody.

Once inside, we put Pannie, the littlest hound of the group, in his crate to settle down. Then Phil tells me the story of getting him at the kennel. Pannie was horrified when Phil went in and leashed him, but in the car Pannie went about sniffing like a crazy dog. Phil explains that Pannie was climbing everywhere. He tried to block him from the front, but Pannie simply climbed over the seat, and as they neared exit 16 on I-81, Pannie crawled right into his lap and sat there, watching his new life unfold in front of him.

I laugh until I cry, but this time they are tears of joy for our newest family member.

During that first year, it's a 24/7 job with Pannie. The most important part of his first step forward is gaining his trust. Once he trusts me, we move on to Phil. I remember that on his second day here, Pannie would not go near Phil. He would find a corner and cower, or he would poop and pee before running into things, just to get away from Phil. Nevertheless, with a lot of love and patience, today Pannie no longer fears Phil.

I also remember days filled with constantly handling Pannie while helping him make decisions. He didn't know how to interact with our Hounds, so I guided him in play and even in simple things like where to lie down to rest. It was a year full of introductions to his new life ahead, but today he knows how to play and where to rest.

Pannie is one of those very special dogs who will forever burn a memory in our hearts. And while we thought we would find Pannie a forever home with some great family, well, we did. But not exactly as we had planned. The forever home Pannie found, with two very devoted humans, was *ours*.

 *Florence Fixx*

Sparkle in Her Eye

Franny came to us needing some work, so to speak. She was underweight, suffering from colitis, and had poor muscle tone due to lack of exercise. Even her back was bowed, but my husband loved her face. When we tried to take her for our daily walks, she would walk 10 feet and stop; she clearly did not understand the point of it. Now, she just motors along, stopping only to sniff something of interest.

Franny warmed up to all of us fairly quickly, taking her place as the boss among our other two dogs. I still remember many of her firsts: the first time she wrestled with her sister, Maggie, and the first time she showed us her stomach. She has made amazing improvements, not just physically, but in her personality as well. After she had been with us a while and her health problems had been addressed, she just became a happier dog. My brother-in-law commented on how he could see a sparkle in her eye that wasn't there before.

When Franny first came to us, she was more attached to me, but now she absolutely adores my husband! She is always the loudest to greet us when we come home from work, and she's the first to hop up on the couch for a snuggle. She has an amazing, funny personality and it adds so much to our group. We love having Franny as part of our family!

 *Courtney Bishop*

Fitness with Fred

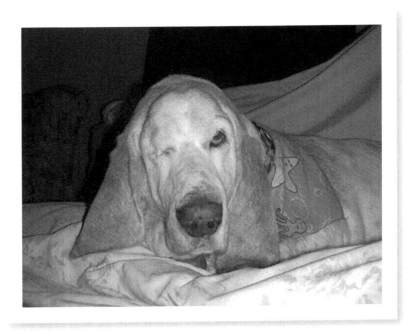

The first time I saw Fred was on the Basset Rescue of the Old Dominion (BROOD) website. It said he was an ORD(owner release dog). I fell in love with his picture: a lemon Basset Hound (I had never heard of such a thing), who appeared to be smiling and very happy. I contacted the person he was living with in Virginia, and she said that he needed someone to be home with him. She also said that after many tests they discovered that Fred had hypothyroidism, but with a pill twice a day, he seemed to be doing fine. He had come into rescue weighing 75 pounds and had lost 10 while on the medication, but the foster mom thought that perhaps he had gained a few pounds back recently.

I just couldn't pass up the chance to adopt Fred, so we made arrangements for me to drive 4½ hours to Virginia to get him. When I walked in the door and saw him, I fell hopelessly in love. He was 70 pounds of Basset Hound. I packed his things into my car, including his bed (which he couldn't fit in), food, water, and food bowls. Then Fred was on his way to his new home. He was an excellent rider in the car, but his weight concerned me since I wasn't sure if I'd be able to get him out of the car! I was pleasantly surprised, however, that with much help from his harness, I got him out.

Fred and I started to work on weight control that very day. We took walks three times a day, though it was obvious that at his previous home he had never been walked. *Ever.*

Fred's former owner said she didn't have time for him but felt that he was very needy. She clearly didn't know much about the breed. Fred was *all* Basset Hound. He loved attention, walks, and especially food. Even so, Fred lost 10 pounds within a couple of months.

Two months after I adopted Fred I noticed that his right eye was cloudy. Not having experience with this before, I took him to my vet. She gave him an exam, including an eye pressure test. She thought that he had glaucoma but wanted me to take him to an ophthalmologist. By luck, there is one 15 minutes from my home, and with the vet calling in the appointment, Fred was able to be seen within two days.

The ophthalmologist, Dr. Bowersox, diagnosed Fred with secondary glaucoma, but more disconcerting was a tumor in

Fred's right eye. The eye had to be removed. I was beside myself. Fred was my "baby," and I didn't want to see him hurting.

Fred had surgery at the end of June. The doctor called me around 1:15 p.m. to let me know that Fred's surgery went extremely well and that I could pick him up tomorrow. As any mom would, I called several more times that day to see how he was doing.

I also called at 5 a.m. the next morning. I wanted him home. They said that the doctor had already seen him and that I could pick him up. A half hour later I was standing in the office waiting for him to come out. He had on an e-collar (one of those plastic lampshades that keeps pets from pawing or licking their surgical sites), but that didn't stop him from greeting me with joy. I was thrilled to see him and couldn't wait to get him home. I had missed him so much and knew he had been through a lot.

Fred was the best post-op patient ever. I wasn't sure how fast he would recover, but he was ready to go for a walk the next day. All this loving and gentle guy wanted was to know that his mom was there for him. He just needed someone who understood the Basset Hound, and more importantly, who understood him. I loved him so much.

Fred didn't play with toys. Just being touched brought him the most joy. He would lie on the floor and wait for me to take my shoes off and rub his belly with my feet. This was our ritual. Fred was the happiest dog I had ever known, and I prayed every day, thanking God for putting him in my life.

When Fred was diagnosed with his tumor, I had only had him a couple of months, yet there were people who told me to put him to sleep. What they didn't know was that Fred had a happy spirit. He wasn't ready to die, which was quite apparent by his quick recovery.

Fred never missed the eye that was removed. He remained the same loving, happy guy he had always been, until he took sick in March of last year. It was just a month after I had to have surgery to remove a tumor from my cheek. I took him to see his vet, Dr. Herrmann, and discovered that Fred had a tumor in his liver. Still, I wanted more tests. A few days later we got an ultrasound of his abdomen, which revealed more tumors in several areas. The vet said that he could perform surgery, but it would only give Fred another two or three months, if he made it at all. The doctor was afraid the tumors in his spleen would burst, which could have happened at any time. If they did, Fred would be in tremendous pain.

On March 18th, Fred went to the Rainbow Bridge after having been with me for just less than two years. It was the most painful day.

I don't think there are enough words to describe Fred and his impact on me and my life. He gave me such great joy. I still miss him every day. I know I was meant to have him share his life with me, or maybe it was the other way around, that I was meant to share my life with him. Anyone who has ever had that special bond with a pet will know exactly what I mean.

 *Dawne Keen*

A Hearty Appetite

When we lost Daisy, our home wasn't the same. We really wanted another bossy Basset with whom we could share our sofa.

I saw Bonnie's picture on the Droopy Basset Hound Rescue website in July 2008. She had this look on her face that screamed, "I can't believe you woke me up to take my picture. I am *not* amused!"

She looked so indignant that I knew she belonged here with us. It was only later I found out that she has a patch of brown hair in the shape of a heart on her chest and a patch of white hair shaped like a heart on her back/shoulder area, and I love hearts!

Once I passed the adoption process, I arranged to meet Bonnie's wonderful foster mom, Diane, in a parking lot halfway between our houses. Diane was torn between keeping her and letting me adopt her. It has to be hard when you foster a dog knowing that one day someone will come along, and you'll have to say goodbye. I was weepy because Bonnie was coming with me, and Diane was weepy because Bonnie was leaving with me. Diane has a huge heart, and I thank her for fostering Bonnie and for being able to let her go.

Initially Bonnie didn't want to be bothered with me, but I was confident that she was meant to live with us, so I signed the papers and took Bonnie home. She was such a good traveler!

It didn't take long for Bonnie to take over the household. The loveseat and couch became hers. (There is one chair in our living room that is supposed to be for people, but one or both of our cats are always on that.) Bonnie gets her needs met by announcing them with a high-pitched whine/cry—that's why we call her Bonnie Boo Hoo sometimes. She is a girl that knows what she wants, and she wants everything *now*!

Bonnie is madly in love with my friend's Chow Chow, Jerry. You can "see" the little hearts come out of Bonnie's eyes when she sees him. They have a lot of fun together and are often seen walking side by side around the yard and through the woods with us.

Bonnie had been rescued from a horse trailer where she had lived with 13 other Basset Hounds. These dogs had been named the "Droopy Dozen." Two years ago at a Droopy fundraiser, Bonnie met up with a few of her old trailer-mates. She met the first one at our hotel. Out of all the dogs in the hospitality suite, Bonnie recognized this one immediately when she came in the room. She looked up, started crying, and walked directly toward this other dog. The other dog responded in kind, and it turned out she was one of the Droopy Dozen as well!

When we got to the actual fundraiser, Bonnie remembered where she was and wanted to leave as soon as we got there. One of the ladies told me that all the rescues act that way. Once the Hounds have their forever homes, they don't want to come back to where they lived after being rescued.

Bonnie will be with us for three years this July. She is a very sweet girl, who loves attention and cookies. She knows how to count, and always expects two after each meal! She still has issues about food, resulting from the time she spent scrapping for food in that horse trailer. We just make sure there is plenty of distance between her and her brother Otto's food station. Between her heart patterns and her love of food, I guess you could say she's got a *hearty* appetite!

 *Betty Harvey*

Anything but a Dud

The day my 90-year-old neighbor and I picked up Dudley it was well over 100 degrees outside. Obese at 90 pounds, Dudley was sitting in the back seat of his owner's Escalade panting up a storm. He appeared distressed. His owner told me that because of a new child, a divorce, and a foreclosure, Dudley fell to the bottom of her priority list. As she handed me his leash, tears rolled down her face.

After several months, Dudley was down to 65 pounds. His Addison's disease (a condition in which a dog's adrenal gland does not produce a sufficient amount of either cortisol or aldosterone) was under control, although expensive to treat. A potential adoptee came to look at him. As she left and I closed the door, I knew Dudley was already home.

Dudley is without a doubt the happiest dog with whom I have ever lived. He loves people, kids, dogs, and cats equally and without discrimination. He hasn't met a person, place, or thing he hasn't loved. He won "happiest tail" at the 2009 Basset Hound Howloween Party because it's always wagging. Dudley enjoys sniffing and sleeping, walking and greeting. He makes everyone's life better.

Two years on, Dudley spends his afternoons napping with my 92-year-old neighbor. He loves his daily walks, greeting anyone and everyone. People can't help but smile at such a big, happy, handsome boy. While still stately, he enjoys running around the house and back yard, enticing the other dogs to play with him. Two minutes later he's lying on his back in the living room, all four feet in the air, sound asleep, snoring up a storm.

I feel blessed to have been given the opportunity to help Dudley because all he has brought me is joy. His owner did the kindest thing she could for him on that sad, hot day, and I have nothing but gratitude for her. And a heart full of love for, and from, Dudley.

 *Leslie Wolcott*

A Letter from Beau

Hello. It's your old friend, Beau. Remember me? I was your companion for the first five years of my life. I'm the cute little puppy you bought at the pet shop that grew into a big boy with a bigger appetite and lots of energy. It seemed like I saw you less and less as time went on. You didn't have as much time for me, and you didn't bother to neuter me or put any ID on my collar. One day I went astray and got into some trouble. I thought you might want to know what happened to me after I escaped from your backyard.

At first it was thrilling to be freed from my lonely existence. I followed my keen Basset Hound nose wherever it led me, but soon I was lost and couldn't find my way home to you. I wandered for quite a while and somehow managed to avoid getting struck by a car, but before I could find you again, I ended up in the pound with a lot of other homeless animals. I didn't care for the smell of that place one bit. I wanted out of there! I was missing you a lot and wondering when you would come to bring me back home with you. Many days passed, but you never came. Time was growing short. Every day I watched others take a last walk down the Gray Mile. They went through a door but never came out again.

Then one day a lady appeared outside my kennel door. I liked her right away, but I'm a friendly guy who likes everyone. I put on my happiest face for her, which wasn't easy after being in that place for so long. She knelt down and poked her fingers through the links of my cage to stroke my head. I sniffed her hand to get her scent. She smelled like a warm bed, good food, naps on the sofa—Home. She looked into my eyes. I looked into hers. I could tell I was making an impression on her, but then she stood up and walked through the front door the way she came in. I was crestfallen. I feared I was doomed like so many others.

After a few minutes, she reappeared with one of the staff, who led me through the door at the end of the corridor. At first I didn't want to follow. That was the same door other dogs disappeared through and never came back, but the lady was coming along, too, so I figured it was okay. It wasn't the nicest place for us to get acquainted, but this was my last chance to win her over, so I did my best. I lay down on the hard concrete floor to let her pet me. Her gentle caress was so comforting. It felt good to get out of my cage for a little while, but the man put me back in the kennel and the lady disappeared through the front door again. I sensed that I might be getting sprung from dog jail, but I couldn't be certain whether fortune would smile on me. When the lady came back once more and talked so kindly to me and even took my photograph, I felt hopeful. She knelt down one more time to pet me. I gave her my biggest dog smile and a last friendly lick on the hand to seal the deal.

It worked! I saw the lady again the day after my neuter surgery. Honestly, it was a small sacrifice to make (well, not that small) for a second chance. She seemed overjoyed to see me, even though we still didn't know each other well. I must have looked pretty silly wearing that stupid Elizabethan collar, but she led me out of the vet's office and helped me into her car. This ride was much different from the last one I'd taken. I had a comfortable cushion to lie upon and soft music played on the car radio. I was a good dog on the long drive to wherever I was headed. I didn't complain or throw up. She kept talking to me in encouraging tones to reassure me all would be well and that I was going to a new home.

I have been in my adoptive home for a month now. I don't want to make you feel bad, but I'm already feeling quite content in my new surroundings. I've had to learn lessons you didn't bother to teach me. I've made some mistakes, but my new family is patient with me in spite of my shortcomings. I love them, and I can tell they love me, too. I have a new dad and a pack mate called Peaches. She's a Basset Hound, too, and also adopted. We adore each other and play together all the time.

The lady who rescued me is a writer. She's taking dictation for me now because dogs can't write letters. I want you to know, in case you ever wonder, that I am well and happy in my new life. I get the best of everything, lots of naps on the sofa and three walks a day. Sometimes I think of you and hope you aren't too sad without me, but I expect you'll find another dog before very long. If so, I hope you will take better care of him than you did of me. If not, I hope he's among the lucky and the few, as I was.

Adieu,

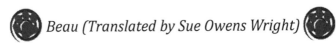 *Beau (Translated by Sue Owens Wright)*

Growing Up Together

Almost a decade ago I adopted my "best boy" Arnie. He had been in foster care for eight months. He really wanted to be the only dog, and mine was the perfect home for him because I was single and didn't have any other pets. He was the perfect dog for me because all he wanted was to give his person unconditional love.

Nevertheless, we had a rocky start at first. One evening as I was leaving, he bit me—hard—on the arm. It was my mistake...I petted him while he was chewing on a bone. That's when I found out he had food aggression! But I was not going to give up that easily. I contacted a trainer, who helped us work through that issue.

Even though I was an adult when I adopted Arnie, I feel like we grew up together. He slowly evolved from a possessive, jumpy dog who didn't trust anyone to a mellow, sweet old man who always knew that no matter how many fosters came and went, he was always going to stay. He came to know that he was always my "best boy."

I went from bad relationship to bad relationship, but Arnie was always there to listen and lick away my tears when my heart was broken. I finally met the man I was going to marry, and luckily he loved my two dogs and my passion for Basset Hound rescue. He promptly built a fence around his pool, for Bassets can't swim, and we all moved in.

Three months before we were to be married, Arnie finally succumbed to his congestive heart failure, which we had been treating for a couple of years. He gave me "the look" that said he was ready to go. I lay on the floor at the vet's office and cuddled him as I said my goodbyes. I remember thinking how ironic it was that we were in the same examining room we had been in the first time I took Arnie to the vet after adopting him. I laughed through my tears as I remembered that he had tried to bite the vet during that visit. I looked at my vet and the vet techs, who had lovingly cared for him for so long and considered him a "nephew" of sorts since he was there so often for treatment, and realized that he had truly come full circle. And so had I.

It is nearly ten years since I adopted Arnie and four years since he passed, but I still volunteer for Arizona Basset Hound Rescue (AZBHR) in his memory. I have two Bassets now, Gracie and Chance, but Arnie will always have a special place in my heart. We taught each other how to trust again. We taught each other the meaning of unconditional love. I miss him every day.

 *Erin Cole*

The Power of Slinging Drool

Herbie the Love Bug's journey to Arizona Basset Hound Rescue (AZBHR) started more than four years ago when he arrived from a puppy mill in another state. He was fostered by Auntie Robin and adopted out for three years, but somehow he found himself in the county shelter, which subsequently returned him to AZBHR. Herbie arrived at my home after having his teeth cleaned (and some removed), being treated for severe ear infections, and suffering through a terrible illness. There were days when I truly thought he was on his last leg, but after many visits to our wonderful vet, Sundance Animal Hospital, Herbie got better. The journey had been a long one.

I adopted Herbie, but about four weeks after his adoption, he woke up one Saturday and couldn't walk. When I tried to help him, he cried out in pain. Like any good mom, I called Pauline, the veterinary tech, and bawled into the receiver. She told me to bring him in as soon as they opened that day.

I carried Herbie to the car, and tears flowed down my face as he cried out in pain. X-rays revealed that Herbie had compressed vertebrae in his neck, which was causing the extreme pain. They gave me medication to help ease his pain, and sent us home with hope that he could come back to his normal self.

I truly believe in the power of prayer and the power of slinging drool from the Hounds. So I posted Herbie's story on my Facebook page and received an overwhelming response. The next day I cried tears of joy because Herbie got up and walked on his own. Between the veterinary help and the outpouring of love, many awesome people helped Herbie recover and walk again without pain.

These days Herbie loves to go for walks even though he has hip dysplasia and compressed vertebrae in his neck. My parents, Herbie's grand-dog-parents, met Herbie when they came for a visit from Wisconsin this year, and they became fast friends. Herbie worked his "love requests" on Grandma for some petting and belly rubs and provided Grandpa with a walking partner. Herbie and Grandpa walked daily with "Momma Kim" and Joanie the Diva, Herbie's sister, whom I had adopted three years earlier. As Grandpa and Herbie came along a bit behind us, Grandpa would say, "Us old guys are coming....at our speed."

Bassets are great therapy, as are many pets, and my parents just loved their time with grand-dog-Hounds, Joanie the Diva and Herbie the Love Bug. I always remind them that if they have anyone to blame for the hours I give to AZBHR, it's them for getting our family a Basset Hound named Wrinkles when I was growing up.

Herbie is approximately nine or ten years old now and still has lots of spunk. At about 3p.m. or so each day, he starts barking as he sits outside my office door to let me know he is hungry. I tell him, "Herbie, it may be five o'clock somewhere, but it's not five o'clock here. Now go lay down." Reluctantly, he walks away but usually comes back a bit later and the cycle starts again!

Herbie is totally a love bug, rolling over when he meets new people to solicit some loving and belly rubs. His grandpa laughed the first time he saw Herbie do the roll over, pretending to be a fallen statue.

Herbie is my handsome boy, mostly black with a bit of brown and white. Never did I think I'd adopt a male dog, as I always preferred females, but I've got to say that Hubba Hubba Herbie is the man in my life now.

My Hounds don't realize it but they are the ones who have rescued me! AROOOO to all the volunteers who help in rescue to save the breed I love...the Basset Hound!

 *Kim A. Bruck*

Liquor Store Love

Three years ago my husband stopped at a liquor store to buy a gift on his way home from work, when a little puppy came up to him wagging her tail. Even though she was small, her flea collar was almost totally embedded in her neck, and her harness was almost overcome by her skin. There was a rope tied to her harness, which she must have chewed through some time ago.

The owner of the store had been feeding her. He helped my husband remove the collar and harness before my husband called me to ask if he could bring her home. I told him he didn't even need to ask!

When he got home with her, I was horrified bywhat I saw. The sores on her neck were so painful looking, and she was so small and hungry. The next day I took her to the vet, where they vaccinated her and cared for her wounds. We never tried to find her owner because it was obvious that she had been neglected.

We named her Molly and planned to help her get well and then find her a home, but we found out that she had a problem with kids and did not trust anyone except us. In our hearts, we knew she was meant to be with us, so we kept her. Three years have now passed, and she is part of our family.

Several people have told us that we should have had her "put to sleep" because she is mean. Granted, she doesn't like children, but she has never hurt anyone and we don't believe her problems are her fault. They are the fault of the human being(s) who abused and neglected her. Molly is a happy dog with us, and we love her like nobody's business.

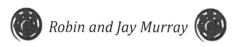 *Robin and Jay Murray*

Basset Break

A Hound Diversion: After my husband was killed on his motorcycle, I was looking for a diversion. I decided to become a foster home for Western PA Droopy Basset Rescue. They asked me to go to a local shelter, pick up a 10-month-old Basset, and foster her until we could find her a home. At the shelter I was informed that she was skittish, but when I got to her cage, I could see why. She was in a large cement room with dogs barking non-stop. I put my hand down, and she kissed it. She was mine. She never made it to the rescue's website. Lexi's only crime: She was a puppy! That was the reason her former owner had surrendered her. Well, she was a wonderful puppy, and four years later she is my rock and my best friend! *-Lisa Uva*

Rewarding Years, Difficult Ears

Humphrey came into my life when I was still reeling from the sudden loss of my job *and* my three dogs—one to cancer, one to complications of valley fever, and one to a rare immunological disorder—all within a four-month period. It was almost too much to bear.

I turned to Arizona Basset Hound Rescue (AZBHR). I had never adopted an adult dog before; I had always raised my dogs from pups, but one look at Humphrey's picture, and I knew he was the one for me. I had become a Basset Hound fan after having my beloved Daisy for eight years. Whereas Daisy was a petite 35 pounds, Humphrey tipped the scales at a solid 75 pounds.

Humphrey happily went with me when I picked him up from his foster home. As we pulled away, he contentedly draped his big body across my lap and seemed to know that he was en route to his forever home. There was only one small problem: Humphrey had been returned to AZBHR (for the third time, poor guy) with ears black with infection. AZBHR doesn't normally adopt dogs out until things like ear infections are cleared up, but when they asked me if his infections would be a problem for me, I said I could handle it. I had cleaned Daisy's ears regularly but still had to deal with an occasional ear infection. How hard could this be? I was about to find out.

Two days after I got him, I took Humphrey to the vet for a follow-up appointment. As long as I took Humphrey to an AZBHR-approved vet, AZBHR would finance his recovery. I was warned on that first visit that in some instances the infection never clears up and the only recourse is to remove the ear canal. Right then I made a silent vow that I would do whatever it took to prevent that from happening.

I was instructed to bring him back that Friday for an ear-flush-sedation. I picked up my groggy pup later that day. The following day Humphrey was vomiting and staggering around to the point that I took him to an emergency clinic that night. Apparently, the procedure had loosened some debris, which had affected his balance and given him motion sickness. They administered fluids and medication, and then I took him home. This was the beginning of a year-long battle including many trips to vets, even to specialists.

During this time, Humphrey continued to bond with our family, but he was really *my* dog. He became my constant companion as my search for a job turned increasingly difficult. Every evening we would walk around the neighborhood, pausing to say hi to passersby. Humphrey's springy step as he trotted down our streets became a familiar sight. People often stopped their vehicles and asked me questions about him or simply smiled.

Occasionally, after doing something that displeased me, Humphrey gave me a pleading look that said, "Please don't get rid of me. I'll be good."

I always assured him that I would never give him up, no matter what.

After repeated ear-flush-sedation procedures proved unsuccessful, we were referred to a veterinarian specialist. One particularly stubborn type of bacteria remained deep inside his ear canals. These bacteria responded to an antibiotic that could only be administered by injection. I couldn't believe what I was hearing! I am a needle-phobic scaredy-cat who faints when I get a shot, but I remembered the vow I made that first vet appointment, so I learned how to give Humphrey injections twice a day for three weeks.

Finally, after a year of ear flushes, pills, and injections, it was time to face the inevitable. We had tried everything. We scheduled surgery for a Total Ear Canal Ablation (TECA) for both ears.

It's almost a year later, and Humphrey is happy, playful, and best of all, pain-free. I never realized how much discomfort he must have been in before his surgery. We have shared quite a journey these past two years. Along the way, I found a job, a best friend, and the strength to handle anything that is thrown my way.

 *Connie Phillips*

Joy-Filled Days

I am not sure Nonni was lost. I think she was out chasing rabbits in the middle of nowhere when the rescue picked her up.

For about six months, I had been looking online for a Basset Hound to adopt, but each time I found one I liked, I would learn that he or she already had found a home. Looking back, though, maybe it was fate because Nonni had not yet shown up.

Most of the other Basset Hounds I had previously viewed were older and fatter than Nonni. She was small for a Basset Hound, weighing only 32 pounds, and she was just two years old. Her foster family said there was nothing medically wrong with her. She was just perfect.

When I went to pick her up, there were several other Basset Hounds in the house, and she was the most timid. I actually wanted the friskier guy, but my daughter insisted that since we came for Nonni, we would go home with Nonni.

Nonni's middle name is now Joy because I adopted her on Christmas Day. She has since become a loving member of our family, although she has some strange habits. She waits for the other dogs to eat before she scarfs down her food, and she runs all over the place, jumping on everything.

She loves the dog park and barking. She is no longer timid, and is as frisky as can be. With her floppy ears, everyone she meets immediately takes a liking to her, and I like to tell them where she is from.

Nonni is our gift of love all year long.

 *Stephanie Rowland*

Heavens to Betsy

Thanks to Arizona Basset Hound Rescue, Betsy came into our home for fostering from a local shelter. Her eyes were bulging and bluish. She was skinny, her nails were curled under into her paw pads, and both of her ears were infected. She was also minus an appetite.

Betsy was diagnosed with ehrlichiosis, commonly known as tick fever, a bacterial blood disease carried by infected ticks. We knew Betsy could not see, and our vet confirmed our suspicions: She had glaucoma. The combination of tick fever and glaucoma do not mix well. Tick fever prevents blood from coagulating, which could cause a dog to bleed to death on the surgical table. Canine glaucoma causes a lot of pain and is not easily controlled with medications; thus, a dog is often better off having his or her diseased eyes removed. However, in Betsy's case, it was too dangerous to do surgery on her eyes, so all we could do was pamper Betsy while the tick fever was being treated.

Three long months passed before our vet said it was safe enough for Betsy to have her eye surgeries. During that time, she would only eat boiled liver and scrambled eggs. At last the day came for her eyes to be removed. Betsy made it through the surgery and immediately started coming alive. She was a hungry and happy girl. She could *baroooo* without her head hurting. We deemed her adoptable.

But oops, it was too soon. The next thing we knew, Betsy had come into a heat cycle. The county shelter had let Betsy's lack of being spayed slip past them. When she finished her cycle, we were relieved. Another two to three weeks later Betsy could be spayed.

Unfortunately, Betsy had another challenge to face. Two weeks after her heat cycle ended, while we were gone for the day, Betsy scratched her face bloody raw. We thought she had allergies and began treating them, but within days Betsy stopped eating and started pacing and panting; she could not get comfortable. Our vet diagnosed Betsy with an infected uterus, a condition called pyometra. The infection was raging throughout her body and she was dying. An emergency spay was performed, but the prognosis was grim.

By now you know Betsy is a survivor, and you would surely expect her to pull through. Well, she did. She overcame her latest ordeal, and within days she was eating like a piggy.

Strangely, Betsy's hair was not growing back after her spay surgery, and she was itching again. This time the diagnosis was hypothyroidism. Now we have to treat her twice a day with one small, inexpensive pill. With its help, her hair has grown back and she does not scratch.

Betsy has overcome a lot of hardship. We are simply amazed to watch her enjoy each day. Every morning she runs out the door with her siblings and listens for us to yell, "Bonk," a signal word to remind her to make a turn from her original path, lest she run into an obstacle. She chases the wild yard bunnies with the rest of her pack and eventually finds her way back through the doggie door to demand breakfast. She eats anything put before her with gusto. Betsy (her daddy calls her Sputnik) knows her way around the house and never misses finding her favorite chair or dog bed. Betsy can always find her mommy, too. We are blessed to have helped this little Basset fight through adversity and blossom into the sweet, loveable girl who was there all along.

Originally Betsy was looking for a temporary home to nurse her back to health. The good news is not only did Betsy get her health back, she became a permanent resident in the same home that fostered her. Who could blame us!

 *Steve and Donna Maschewski*

Spice Girls

This story began in January three years ago. Our family has always had three Basset Hounds, but we were down to two after losing Nutmeg in November of the previous year. She was 14 years old, and prior to that we had lost her mother, Cinnamon, at age 14. Do you see a trend here? The remaining two dogs were Hoops (a.k.a. Rosemary), age 10, and Thyme, age 6. Our family felt incomplete.

We started looking for another Basset Hound and found Ellie with a rescue group. She was a one- or two-year-old tri-color Basset Hound weighing in at a mere 25 pounds. Her eyes and innocent look made my heart melt. Her bio said she was found wandering the streets down near New Philadelphia, Ohio, where she had probably been dumped out of a car. The dog catcher took her to the pound, where she was days from being euthanized. That's when Kim, from the rescue, picked her up and took her to her home as a foster dog.

I called to inquire about Ellie, and they said that she was already pending adoption. I was brokenhearted because I had fallen in love with her bio and pictures. I continued looking, but none seemed to compare with Ellie.

Then, on a cold, snowy evening in early January, about two weeks after inquiring about Ellie, the phone rang. It was Kim from the rescue. She asked me, "Are you still interested in adopting Ellie? The adoption fell through with the previous family."

I said, "Absolutely!"

We arranged for Ellie to visit our home in Akron, Ohio, the following weekend. We had to be sure Hoops and Thyme liked her. That Saturday afternoon, Kim and her husband brought Ellie for her visit. It was love at first sight for Greg and me and also for Hoops and Thyme. All the dogs ran around the house and played with toys. The visit lasted about an hour, during which time Kim and her husband inspected our home to ensure it would be a safe environment for Ellie. We showed them the doggy doors, the fenced yard, and the doggy ramp onto the bed. Kim looked at us and said, "I can't think of a better home for Ellie!"

Those were the best words I had ever heard, and the rest is history. We changed her name to a spice, Ginger, to stick with our "Spice Girls" theme. She is now about four years old and weighs in at 68 pounds. She loves everyone she meets and gets along with the other pups. She is one of the best things to have happened to us. She sleeps with us and the other pups in the bed. She is a gem, and I can't imagine life without her.

 *Lisa Hensley*

A Special Old Boy

I liked showing Basset Hounds. I had three of my own, and while I had been helping with transport and fundraising, I never planned on fostering Bassets. Then I received a call to check out a senior Basset in my area who needed a new home.

I met his owners, gave them the surrender paperwork to review, and told them I would see if we had a foster home open, as I myself didn't foster. Then I met Alex... He looked up at me with eyes slightly cloudy, a heavy-lipped muzzle, a beautiful head, and front legs that faced east and west. He was a faded red-and-white Hound with a deep "woof." There was something about this old boy...

On my way home, Alex's face stayed in my mind. By the next day I decided to bring Alex to my house until a foster home opened up. As soon as he heard the collar and leash when I went to pick him up, he started woofing excitedly. It turned out Alex loved going for car rides. When we left that day, he woofed nonstop and barely looked back.

I had been told he had separation anxiety, but I wasn't concerned, thinking it no big deal. At home I introduced him to our dogs and the doggy door. He seemed to settle in fine. But that night, as I went to go to sleep, Alex became unglued and started shaking, trembling, panting, crying, pacing, and peeing. I spent the night on the floor with him, thinking the first night here would be the worst and he'd settle in. After a week of sleeping on the floor with him, I took him upstairs to our bed.

We tried anti-anxiety drugs with unimpressive results. In my herbal books I read about Valerian Root capsules, and they worked miracles. He still got anxious when we left home, but his anxiety was manageable. Alex was a real sweetheart.

In the first year he was with me (yes, I said *year*), I received a few inquires about him. Each time I explained what a sweet boy he was, how he loved to go places and got along with other pets well (although cats were so fun to chase!). Then I would explain about the separation anxiety and his chronic eye and ear problems. I'd say he did pretty well with not peeing in the house if you had a doggy door—granted sometimes he would get his front half out the dog door and start peeing, but...I'd say, "You really need to meet this boy. There is just something about him. Did I mention he was a bit hard of hearing? And just a touch senile?"

For some reason no one was lining up to adopt this 10-year-old. It was hard to understand why...

After 18 months, I decided Alex would stay with us. He was a bit weak in the rear, but got around fine. We joked that he came with one foot in the grave, but like a Timex, he kept on ticking. Alex was a strange old boy. His favorite and only game was to get a rawhide chewy and have you stand over him and try to take it away from him, saying, "I'm gonna get it!"

He'd harmlessly growl and snap. When he tired of this game, he would contentedly lie down and chew on his rawhide.

Alex slowly lost of control of his rear end, and the first time he took a tumble down our stairs was the last time he slept upstairs. But by then he was a bit more senile and adjusted well to the change.

Although he went deaf and could only see shadows, his old nose still worked beautifully. Alex loved bread with a passion. He could be sound asleep, and if I had a sandwich in another room, his old head would almost fly up, nostrils wide, snuffling the air. He would also snuffle the bottom of the door when I left. From our breezeway it sounded like the door was breathing. It was always funny to see the look on a visitor's face the first time they heard it.

Alex always gave me little kisses when I put my face to his muzzle. If he was stressed or unsure, all I had to do was kiss him on the nose and let him sniff and kiss me, and he would calm right down.

Alex was with me for almost three years. I adored this old boy with all my heart, and when it was his time to go, he went in my arms. Since that time I have fostered over 130 Basset Hounds. Alex never knew what he started. Alex showed me how special senior Basset Hounds are and how much they can teach us about enjoying each moment in life. Seniors are still my favorite fosters.

 *Judy Helfferich*

Like a Rose Blossom

The first thing we noticed about Rosie was her big, brown eyes. She was a Basset-mix; quite small; full of light, brown, wiry fur; and very reserved. She was silent and moved very slowly and deliberately. She seemed so sad and worse than afraid—kind of lethargic—and we didn't perceive much feeling coming from her at all. She was dumped at a high-kill shelter in the South, and a caring employee called the Looziana Basset Rescue (LBR).

When we picked up Rosie from Metairie Small Animal Hospital, she looked at us with her sad eyes, and each of us reached out to scratch and pet her with a big smile. I think I saw life come into those windows to her soul, which is what we always called her eyes. She didn't wag her tail but stood there letting us pet her. She did lean into my scratches behind her ears and lifted up her leg so I could scratch her underarms.

I think she was slowly warming up to us and trusting us a little at a time.

I decided she needed a full name, so we anointed her Rosie Claire Oliver. Claire is the name of my favorite doll.

My two-year-old Basset/Beagle, Jenni, jumped at the idea of having a new friend, and when she saw Rosie, she knew she had a friend for life. Rosie had to be treated for severe heartworm and couldn't play very much, so Jenni was a little disappointed. During that time, we noticed Rosie warming up to Jenni; they would lie together, touching, on the sofa. As time went on, we let Rosie play a little, and Rosie started following Jenni outside to do her business. Rosie learned a lot of good habits from Jenni.

Finally, we were told Rosie was heartworm-free. She continued to follow Jenni around, and she started wagging her tail when we approached. We were thrilled the first time she looked up for us to pet her with sparkle in her eyes. When we would say her name, she would wag her tail in circles. For a long time, she would deliberately walk around the den and lie in one place.

One day, a few weeks after we had her, Jenni heard a truck pass the front of the house and down the street. Jenni barked as usual, and ran to the window. Rosie lifted her head, saw Jenni run off, and jumped up and ran to the window to look out with Jenni. I remember that moment very well, as it was the first time we saw Rosie run.

Later Rosie started joining us in games. She chased balls, wrestled with Jenni, and came to us looking to cuddle. She was a special and sweet dog, who seemed to be happy staying with us. Each of us fell in love with Rosie, and we couldn't remember not having her live with us. We couldn't imagine not having her as our special girl.

Unfortunately, probably because of the severity of the heartworms, Rosie's immune system didn't fully recover, and she contracted cancer. Over a few weeks, her activity level slowed, and she gradually stopped eating. The last thing we wanted was for Rosie to suffer, but it was very hard to take her to the vet to be put to sleep.

Dr. Brian at the animal hospital had seen her a few times over the months and said she seemed so happy and beautiful while she was with us. We believe her last weeks were the happiest time she ever had. Everyone says that we gave her something to live for, and we're so glad to have given her a home and a happy life. Daddy put her ashes in a very special place in the family room where I walk by and think of her every day. I will always remember her and miss her. Our Rosie will always have a special place in our hearts.

 *Mary Beth Oliver (Age 12)*

Basset Hound Manners and Things

My husband had always wanted a Basset Hound. Eight years ago, the Basset girl we were looking at had been adopted, but we were told the shelter had another Basset Hound available. When I met him, I was a little taken aback by how sad, lonely, and unkempt Kipper was. Nevertheless, we took a chance on him, and he turned out to be a wonderful and loyal boy.

Two years ago, we drove across the country to move to Arizona. Once we settled in, we wanted Kipper to have Basset Hound siblings, so we adopted Abbigale and Paula from Arizona Basset Hound Rescue (AZBHR). We then learned about AZBR's great need for foster homes, so we gave fostering a try.

Kipper has been very tolerant and accepting of the 10 foster Basset Hounds that have come and gone. He has taught them Basset Hound manners and how to do Basset Hound things.

At 12-years-old, Kipper has started to slow down, but he continues to love his walks, treats, and cuddle time. He has learned that I will give him what he wants; all he needs to do is give me that special Basset Hound look and bark.

Although we will be sad when it is Kipper's time to cross the Rainbow Bridge, we will never forget how much love and enjoyment he has brought to our lives.

 *Carrie Diana*

6½ Weeks of Bliss

An email went out telling the story about Naomi, whose family had discarded her in a dumpster at a McDonald's in the east valley of Phoenix. It seems the manager saw a couple walk away from the dumpster, so he went over to see what they had put inside. Imagine his surprise to find a sweet, petite, Basset Hound!

He called animal control, who then contacted Arizona Basset Hound Rescue (AZBHR) to take her in. The poor girl was very sick, and she couldn't walk on one of her legs. The vet determined that Naomi (named by AZBHR), had terminal cancer in her bone and spleen. Her time on this earth was limited, so she would have to be a permanent foster in a home with people who would help her to the Rainbow Bridge when it was her time.

Her story tugged at my heart. It was only days before Christmas, and I knew Naomi needed someone to love on her. Naomi lived happily with me for 6½ weeks, during which time she got lots of belly rubs, cuddles, steak dinners, and treats. Loving and more loving were the orders of the day.

Then, sadly, that fateful day came, when no amount of pain medication could help Naomi, and I knew I had to say goodbye. Naomi and I headed to the vet's office, but not until after we stopped at McDonald's for the cheeseburger she had been promised. I laughed at her as she picked off the bread and ate the meat, and I told her that where she was going, she wouldn't have to worry about her weight, and she could eat the bread, too.

Naomi was so sweet and gentle. I held her in my arms and cried as I said goodbye to her with words reassuring her that many others would be at the Rainbow Bridge to meet her, and she would be pain free forever.

Fly free, sweet Naomi! Foster Momma Kim loves you and misses you!

 *Kim A. Bruck*

Short but Sweet

I have a Basset Hound who is now almost nine years old. I got him from Golden Gate Basset Rescue and decided that he needed a companion. Since Buddy had been such a wonderful addition to our family, I decided to again look up adoptable dogs to find him a best friend. I came across "Snuggles," with ears that touched the ground. He looked almost identical to my Buddy, so I had to find out all about him. It turned out he was rescued from a neglectful backyard breeder. He was so sick that he had an extended stay at a local vet, who loved him so much they said they could have kept him. We felt lucky to have found him.

After discussing this dog with the rescue, we drove for three hours to meet him at an adoption event and bring this sweet puppy home. He was wobbly on his feet and tripped on his ears; it was an adorable sight. I named him Copper, and upon arriving at our home, our older Basset Hound took to him instantly, as did my family. He obviously belonged with us.

A week later I took Copper to the vet for a checkup. The vet was concerned that he was too thin for his age and wanted to run some tests. Blood tests showed that Copper had a massive infection. The vet couldn't tell for sure, but it looked like it was in his lungs. The vet told me that Copper would probably be a special needs dog his whole life, and we would probably be limited on a lot of things we could do with him. I gladly took on the challenge.

With the help of antibiotics, Copper gained strength. Two weeks passed, and Copper seemed to be making progress. He developed a healthy appetite and became quite the nippy, rambunctious pup. He gained about eight pounds, which made him look like a normal pup his age. My little new best friend became my shadow; anywhere I went, Copper went. He was so lovey and affectionate, crawling up on the couch to lie on Buddy, as if he were Buddy's pup. I was so happy the two liked each other, and I kept remarking about how much they looked alike. It was like seeing Buddy when he was a puppy. What a treat that was, since I didn't know Buddy as a puppy because he was two when we adopted him.

Buddy and Copper were adorable together, and Copper was making great strides. Copper's checkup was on the horizon, and I couldn't wait for our vet to see how great he was looking. But one Monday afternoon before he could visit his vet and show off his great progress, I went out to the back yard and found Copper lying by a swing. He was out sunning like he loved to each afternoon, only this time it looked like something was wrong. I wrapped him in a towel and took him to the emergency clinic. The vet told me that Copper had a seizure and ran some more tests to figure out what had happened. It was distemper, which could have been prevented had his previous owner provided basic puppy vaccinations.

I asked them to do whatever they could to save him. The vet wanted to keep him overnight. Before leaving, I checked on Copper one last time to tell him I loved him and that I would see him in the morning after I got off from work. He looked all right, and I felt good leaving the clinic. When I called a few hours later to check on Copper before I went to work that night, the nurse said he was doing really well. I could pick him up around 10 p.m. if I wanted to, and they would send him home with some medications.

I was just about to get into my car to go get Copper when the clinic called me with horrible news. Copper had passed away. I was absolutely devastated. The vet talked to me and reminded me how much I fought for Copper and how much love I gave him during the short time I had had him. He said how lucky Copper was to have had a family like us. I still cried for days, but finally I decided that instead of being sad, I would have a celebration ceremony for Copper. My family got together, and we all shared pictures and happy stories of

Copper. We made a little movie about all the funny things I saw Copper do.

I felt better in realizing that he came into our lives so that he could learn what love was and what a family felt like before he went to heaven. He passed away nearly three years ago, yet I still turn around sometimes because it feels like he is standing right behind me, following me to see what I am doing. I know that Copper is not physically here with me, but he has a special place in my heart, which he will occupy forever.

Even though he is gone, Copper will always be a member of our family. I'm so glad that we had the opportunity to have him in our lives.

 *Jessica Manthei*

The Chase

I had my heart set on getting a Labrador Retriever. What I ended up with was a mix: Lab, Basset Hound, and possibly Border Collie. Having adopted her at six weeks old, we didn't have a clue as to what she would look or act like when fully grown, but Oreo ended up looking like a Lab with a Basset Hound body. Her personality, however, was all Basset!

Fourteen years later when we had to say good-bye, I was grief-stricken. I never wanted to go through that experience again, but I also knew I had to have a dog(s) in my life. I decided I wanted to be a foster parent for a Basset Hound rescue. I thought maybe fostering would keep me from getting attached and would allow me to help a needy Basset Hound by providing a temporary home for him or her.

Kaiser entered our lives a year ago when Basset Rescue of the Old Dominion (BROOD) asked me if I would take him in as a foster. He had been surrendered to a shelter by his family, who had to move into an apartment and could no longer keep him.

My husband and I drove to Maryland to pick him up from the kennel. When we arrived, we immediately picked him out from the group of Bassets barking and carrying on at the sight of visitors. Kaiser was huge, weighing 76 pounds. He was also very strong. He greeted us as if he knew that our relationship would be long-term. Upon getting into the car, he appeared very excited about his new adventure, but as soon as we started driving away, he began howling. I wondered what he was trying to tell us, but after 45 minutes of continuous howling, I was at a loss. I thought to myself, "Oh boy. What have I gotten myself into?"

I prayed that Kaiser wouldn't howl the entire ride home, which was about 2½ hours long. Luckily, he finally settled down after wearing himself out.

At home we let Kaiser explore his new surroundings. Everything was going better than I had anticipated; that is, until he saw the neighbor's cat. All hell broke loose. I thought he was either going to go through the fence or dig under it to escape. I tried to get him back inside, but he snapped at me.

When we finally got him in and calmed down, I realized I was going to need help with his behavior. This was further impressed upon me when the following day on our walk, one minute he was attached to the leash, and the next minute he was free and running. Now, I know the worst thing anyone can do to capture a loose dog is to run after him, but Kaiser was not going to listen to a stranger calling him, and there was no way I could get his attention. I ran and ran until I thought my heart was going to burst, but I was finally rewarded with being able to tackle him on my neighbor's lawn. Getting him back home was a nightmare. Thinking about it afterward, though, I have to laugh. Can you imagine the neighbors looking out their windows and seeing this short, fat dog running down the road with this old, fat lady in hot pursuit?

Kaiser was, and still is at times, a challenge. He did have some issues, but wouldn't you if your family deserted you? We ultimately couldn't part with him and quickly became "foster failures," meaning that we kept him and didn't find him another home.

Today Kaiser is like a different dog. After losing 20 pounds, he is fit, happy, and secure. These days we ask him to howl for us. He puts a smile on our faces every day and has helped us through the most difficult time in our lives. He hasn't replaced our beloved Oreo; she will always be in our hearts, but he has put joy back into our lives and given us a reason to open our hearts once again. That's our boy!

 *Christina DePierro*

Basset Break

The Pup I Couldn't Pass Up: When visiting my daughter, Kelli, in Florida, we went to a pet supply store that had dogs available for adoption. I walked around a corner, and Molly was there. She reared up with her front paws on my shoulders, gave me a sweet kiss, and I fell in love. Kelli always says Molly picked me. Since my daughter was coming to visit us in a few weeks and I had flown down, I asked if she could foster Molly and then bring her home to me when she came. She agreed and brought her back to me in about a month. Molly has been my baby girl ever since. -*Marilynn Nall*

Sneaky Snacks: One day I came home from work and found pieces of foil on my kitchen floor. The night before I had made garlic bread to go with a pasta sauce I had cooking in my crock pot. I had assumed that Phoebe, my Basset Hound, had gotten on my counter again. That night I was in bed reading, and I thought I heard her chewing on something. I got up and found out that she carried the garlic bread piece by piece up the stairs and had hidden it in my closet. She had stored it there and was using it for snacks!-*Barbara Crawford*

For Whom the Belle Rolls

When I first heard about the "Droopy Dozen," as they would forever be called, I was outraged. They had lived their lives in a horse trailer, sometimes going days without food or water. When Mark and I were asked to foster not one but two of the dogs rescued from this horrific situation, I was overjoyed!

In April we brought home Bonnie and Belle. Bonnie was adopted a few months later, but Belle would take a little longer. Saying she was shy was an understatement. She was afraid of everything around her, but people were her biggest fear. During the first few months, she spent a lot of time in her crate looking out at the world or pretending it wasn't there. Slowly she began to trust me, and we started to make some progress, but I soon realized it would be a very long road. It took a full year before she was housetrained.

When Belle met new people, she would cower and try to get as far away from them as she possibly could. I felt sure I could change that, and slowly I did. At home, in her own environment, the true Belle began to come out. If she wasn't tearing around and making us laugh, she was cuddled up next to us, pushing us out of bed.

People began expressing interest in adopting Belle, but as soon as they saw her fearful behaviors, they were turned off. Who wants a dog you can't get next to or even make eye contact with? Eventually we found what we thought would be the perfect home for Belle, and after 14 months of fostering, we said goodbye to the last of the Droopy Dozen to be adopted. I cried halfway home.

For the next couple of weeks, I couldn't shake the feeling that something wasn't right. I thought perhaps I just missed my little Belle. I had never had such a hard time giving up a foster, and my answer came with a phone call informing me that Belle was coming back. She was not adjusting to her new family, and they felt it was not going to work out, even though they said they thought love would fix her problems.

Belle came back to us and immediately took up where she left off, no worse for the wear. I promised her she would never have to leave again as I filled out the adoption application.

I learned something from this experience. Dogs and people are who they are for a reason, and we must accept them for that. To do otherwise is a disservice not only to them but to ourselves as well. As much as I would love Belle to be like other dogs and go everywhere with me, she is who she is, and I think I love her even more for that very reason.

 *Diane Burns*

The Forever Foster

When my husband's son and daughter-in-law divorced, we inherited their Basset-mix, Odie. Odie was a rescued Hound who had originally come from one of the shelters in Florida. At the time, I could never imagine the impact this Hound would make on our lives.

We loved Odie. He made us see that if one Basset Hound was good, two must be better. One night at work I had too much time on my hands, and I stumbled across Suncoast Basset Rescue's website. I pulled up the "Foster a Basset" form, looked at it closely, and thought, "I can do this."

I filled out the form and submitted it. Within a week we were approved and we received our first foster, Brandy.

Life was good; we had two Basset Hounds. We had a vacation coming up, and we intended for the Hounds to accompany us on it. However, right before we were leaving, we received a call from Suncoast's adoption coordinator, Amy, about a family who was interested in Brandy. Without hesitation, my husband informed Amy that Brandy wasn't going anywhere because we were taking her on vacation with us. Of course, Brandy was ours from that point on.

Jasmine was our next foster failure. She was nine months old and heartworm positive when she came to us. She had been relinquished to Suncoast by two college students who had originally named her Ammo.

Within just a few weeks of getting Jasmine, Suncoast asked us to foster Dunker. Dunker was an owner relinquish, too. His mom was getting a divorce and felt she couldn't take care of him any longer. Dunker reminded us of Baby Huey, a fictional baby duckling cartoon character, who was big and clumsy and always had a confused expression on his face—just like Dunk. My husband instantly fell in love with him. Now my husband was insisting we adopt two more Basset Hounds. Of course, if you ask him, he will tell you that I was the one who insisted we adopt them.

Fosters came and went for a few months, and then we got Lucy. Lucy was also an owner relinquish. She had spent the first nine months of her life tied up on a porch, and her feet had never touched grass.

A couple weeks later we got Chrissy, who was also an owner relinquish. She was seven months old and a terrible barker. No matter how hard we tried, we couldn't get Lucy housetrained, and we couldn't get Chrissy to stop barking. After several months their issues hadn't gotten any better.

I loved these two girls and didn't want to see them go from one home to another unless we could find a home that could deal with their issues. So, you guessed it. Chrissy and Lucy became our fourth and fifth foster failures.

Life with the Basset Hounds can be a challenge sometimes, but it's also been extremely fun and rewarding. They have brought us love and laughter and an inner peace that you can only get from a beloved pet. Becoming a "foster" home for Suncoast Basset Rescue is one of the best things that has ever happened in my life.

 *Kitty Workman*

Solace

Raja came into our lives 2½ years ago. I had received an email from the Arizona Basset Hound Rescue about a four- or five-month-old female Basset-mix, who was in Tucson, Arizona, with a family that had six other dogs and four children. They were in way over their heads with this puppy named Baby. I opened the email with great caution, as I always do because I am an avid dog lover and to hear stories about dogs who fall victim to families that can no longer keep them tears me apart.

This particular dog caught my eye. Baby was shown sitting outside on a door mat that looked like it was dragged through the mill. All I could see was this sad look in her eyes that said, "Help! I sleep on this torn dirty mat, and I'm not wanted here."

I immediately forwarded the email to my husband, and not more than two minutes later, my husband said, "Let's go get her."

I was excited. We picked her up that Saturday after she was fixed, and she has been a pleasure to have in our family ever since. Her fur is a gorgeous black, different from your ordinary Basset-mix. We found out that she had a broken tail, and we think it's from someone closing a door on it. We changed her name from Baby to Raja, as she didn't look like a Baby to us.

Raja came into our lives at the perfect time. I already had two other dogs, Lucy and Ricky. Lucy was nine years old, and Ricky was eight. Lucy and Ricky have been my rocks and have gotten me through a lot. I was worried about how Raja would fit in and how Lucy and Ricky would accept the new puppy. Progress was slow, but we became a happy family.

Several months later, Lucy started acting strangely. She was slowly starting to lose the use of her rear legs. We brought her to the vet, who referred us to a neurologist. The neurologist told us she needed back surgery, but the cost would be substantial. I was at a loss. My husband knew I had to spend the money because I thought Lucy had more fight in her, but tragically, $7,000 and three months later, we found out Lucy had lymphoma. We were devastated. Perhaps the back surgery had triggered something?

I had never lost a dog, and losing Lucy was like having my heart torn out. No amount money was going to save her at that point, and I wasn't about to put her through chemotherapy. Lucy lasted about another month before we knew it was time. Raja and Ricky said their goodbyes, and we kissed our Lucy for the last time. I keep Lucy's ashes in my "I Love Lucy" cookie jar on a special shelf.

Since Lucy's passing, Raja and Ricky have bonded more than I could ever have imagined. My husband and I see many characteristics of Lucy in Raja, things Lucy did that Raja does now. I truly believe that Lucy gave her blessing to have Raja become part of our family before she left us, and that even though Ricky misses her because they were a bonded pair since birth, he's gotten over her passing much more easily because of Raja's presence.

 *Stacey and Troy Lent*

Bobbing Buddy

One evening my husband and I were renewing our weary bones in the hot tub when we saw Buddy, our Basset Hound, go flying through the doggie door into the house. We followed him in and noticed he was acting strangely. Panic took over when I saw a Colorado River Toad in the middle of the living room. We knew the toad was poisonous, so we flew into action. My husband scooped up the toad, while I grabbed Buddy and headed for the hose to rinse out his mouth. After less than a minute, Buddy wanted nothing to do with the hose.

Knowing we had 15 more minutes of rinsing to do, we had to come up with a new plan. John decided food would be the incentive. He tossed a little kernel of food into Buddy's large water bowl and Buddy, known to never pass up food, took a nosedive into the water. John repeated the game, and Buddy suddenly loved "bobbing for apples" until we were convinced all the potential poison was gone. Buddy's head was completely soaked, and the kitchen floor was a pool of water, but Buddy had bobbed for some great, "life-saving" treats and had treated us with a comical water stunt, too.

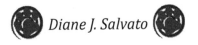 *Diane J. Salvato*

Not Just a Number

Thelma Lou started her life as "just a number" in an Arizona puppy mill, with little to no human contact. Before I welcomed her into my home two years ago, she was a very frightened dog who was released from the mill to Arizona Basset Hound Rescue with a group of other dogs from the same mill. Her life up to that point consisted of living outdoors in a fenced-in area, on concrete or dirt, with limited shelter, food, and water.

When she came home with me, she ran to a corner of the backyard and would not come near anyone or into the house.

For days she paced the back area of the yard or stayed in the corner for hours and hours, until I went to bed. Then, sometime during the night, when she thought it was safe, she would come into the house. This was how things went for many, many days. I didn't think I would ever be able to get close to her; it was going to be a long road ahead for both of us. She had never been inside a house before, so any loud noises, including those on TV programs, would send her bolting out to the backyard.

As the days went on, I noticed Thelma Lou getting more and more lethargic. She hardly moved from the corners in the house—her safe spots. I brought her to the vet after seeing this abnormal behavior, and she was diagnosed with a very bad case of kennel cough. I gave her antibiotics, but she still became progressively sicker. Her kennel cough had developed into pneumonia, and she had to stay several days at the vet. We were not even sure if she was going to survive.

Finally, she took a turn for the better and was able to come back home. Due to the constant nursing and attention I had been giving her, we had a much stronger bond when she came back. She still wanted nothing to do with anyone else, but she tolerated me. She also did well with the other Basset Hounds in the house.

I began crate-training her and discovered that she felt much more secure in her crate. She spent a lot of her time in there as she slowly became acclimated to her new world, and today she seldom goes in there at all. Even so, I think it makes her feel secure to know it is there for her if she needs it. Time and patience were the key in working with her. Each day was, and sometimes still is, like "Groundhog Day" for her, as many times she forgets the progress from the previous day and we have to start over again.

Little by little, day by day, Thelma Lou and I are making "baby steps" progress. She is very relaxed when it's just us, at which times she sleeps belly-up on the couch and snores like a lawnmower! Her favorite place is in my lap, when we both take an afternoon nap together, and she plays like a puppy with all the dog toys.

I recognize that Thelma Lou might never be a "normal" dog. She has lots of baggage and issues from her days in the puppy mill. But when I look back and see the progress she has made, it makes me smile and love her all the more, for her finally trusting and loving me back, in her own unique and special way. She now gets to be a spoiled and pampered little girl for the rest of her days. I think she deserves nothing less.

 *Lenora Skog*

News Hound

I've had Basset Hounds of both genders in the past, and when I was down to two girl Hounds, I found myself missing having a boy in the family. We'd had a great previous experience with Looziana Basset Rescue (LBR) when we adopted our Louise, so I decided I'd return to find my boy.

I found Sherman on the LBR website, and it was love at first sight. He just had that certain look in his eye, and I knew he was destined to be our dog. He came to LBR after being pulled from a New Orleans shelter at approximately one year of age. He was extremely emaciated and undergoing treatment for heartworm disease, so he could not be cleared for adoption yet. No problem! We decided to foster him until that time came.

He spent his first two months with us mostly resting in his crate. During that time he endured several overnight stays in the hospital for his heartworm treatments. When at our home, we filled his tummy several times a day with lots of nutritious food, so he could gain some much-needed weight.

After his last treatment, we finalized his adoption, and today, at just over two years old, Sherman is a big, smooshy, happy, healthy, handsome boy of nearly 60 pounds! He has a great outlook on life, and he doesn't have a mean bone in his body. He's always ready to play with us, the girl Hounds, or his toys. He also loves to hang out with his dad, watching the news and football or playing chef's assistant. Belly rubs and rumpy scratches are also a big priority.

We love Sherman to bits and just can't imagine why someone else tossed him out like yesterday's news. He means the world to us and will be a headliner in our lives for the rest of his days.

 *Debbie Berthelot*

A Little Sunshine

Sunshine was rescued from a life as a breeder. Her first five years must have been hell. She came to us not knowing how to be a dog! I'd never had a dog who didn't know how to chase a ball, do "mad dog" through the house after a bath, or even beg for food, but that was Sunshine.

The first time I saw that little Basset Hound, she was anything but "sunny." Her tail was firmly planted between her legs, and she stared pointedly at the ground in front of her. I held a treat under her nose, and she made no attempt to even sniff it. This little girl was traumatized!

My sister and I fell in love with her the first time she lifted her head and looked at us with those big, brown eyes. That was almost five months ago. Her first few weeks with us were rough. Shortly after she came to live with us, we discovered a tumor on her side. She underwent surgery, leaving a huge incision and stitches on her side. An anxious weekend of waiting brought the happy news that the tumor was benign. But now our little ball of fear was also in terrible pain.

We spent several nights lying on the floor next to her bed, trying to comfort her. We hired a dog trainer to help us learn how to socialize Sunny and bring her out of her haze of pain and fear. For hours on end, we petted her, talked to her, and practiced the techniques given to us by the trainer. Slowly, Sunny started to raise that tail on walks, sniff our hands, and look about her. One morning she started playing with a sock! Heavens above, we now give her socks to play with all the time. In any other house, she might hear, "Bad dog," for stealing socks, but we figure it's a small price to pay to see her running around, growling, and throwing the sock into the air before biting it and shaking it around her head.

Sunny now has two jobs: chase the squirrels out of the yard and take us for walks. She's terrible at the first job because she seems to be afraid of squirrels. She's very good at the second job. Every morning she waits patiently while her human pack eats breakfast and plays on those computer things. Then, she'll start running up and down the hall, "talking" to us to let us know it is time for a walk. If we don't move fast enough, she escalates to racing through the entire house, doing those funny little hound-dog hops that Basset Hounds are so good at. Sometimes we're laughing so hard it's difficult to put our shoes on.

We've taken Sunny on a couple of road trips. I think her favorite places to get out and have a good "sniffums" sessions were Mt. Lassen National Forest, Lake Tahoe, and Cayucos Beach in California. A romp on the beach definitely got her up and moving. There were so many new things to discover, so many things to chase.

This has been a voyage of discovery for both dog and humans. Watching this little girl discover new things—much like a puppy—after five years of sensory deprivation is an absolute joy. And, taking Sunshine on walks has opened up an entirely new part of our town to us. We've been to places we previously passed by for years and met people we've lived next to for years, whom we wouldn't have otherwise known.

Sunshine has come a long way from that little huddled bundle of fear, and she still has a way to go. People ask me what the secret of success has been with her, and I always answer that it's the power of love. Who could resist loving this little being?

As a friend of mine said upon meeting Sunny, "Everybody needs a little Sunshine in their lives."

 *Doris Smith*

Tears and Cheers

W hat can you say about a five-year-old Basset Hound who died? That she was beautiful and brave? That she loved belly rubs, baby feet, ice cream, and a Red Flyer wagon? That her life was ending when we came together, but in those six remaining months, she would move many to tears *and* to cheers? She was amazing.

With less than a week remaining until Christmas, I was elated when my foster Basset Hound Abby was adopted into her forever home. Woohoo! I would spend Christmas with family and upon returning to my cozy little townhome in Dumfries, Virginia, would request another foster Basset Hound. Having become a foster home for BROOD (Basset Rescue of the Old Dominion) earlier that year, I found that both I and my kind-hearted Basset Hound, Hoover, enjoyed our temporary house guests. We both had more than enough love and nurturing to share as each sad-eyed Basset Hound, wounded in numerous ways, slipped into our routine, our bed, and our hearts.

December 23rd brought a phone call about a staggering Basset Hound dropped off at the overflowing holding kennel. She was a confused, frightened, and severely impaired little girl, who desperately needed to be in a quiet and attentive home. So while everyone else was in the countdown to the final 24 hours of Christmas, we were on the countdown to getting our new foster dog, Pecos, and before day's end, she was whisked from the kennel chaos to the warm bath and bed our home could provide. Hoover, with his welcoming watchful eye, undoubtedly was happy that Christmas would now be spent at home with a new foster.

Pecos' affliction was a mystery, and her relinquishing family provided little historical information. Her saving grace was the apparent lack of pain. She wobbled when she walked, with an odd, over-reaching step, and any movement appeared to be a challenge. She valiantly staggered toward the door when responding to nature's call, but outdoor potty runs were impossible in her condition. I quickly learned to express her bladder, stimulate bowel movement, and carefully time her meals. Pecos adapted to saucy, padded denim britches, and we seemed to have things under control.

The search for a diagnosis and a plan of treatment took us to several specialists. Pecos had blood tests, X-rays, a spinal tap, an MRI, rehab therapy, acupuncture, and holistic treatments. Then we received the devastating diagnosis: Her brain and spine were affected by neurological distemper, undoubtedly having been latent in her body from earlier survival of the disease, which, by the way, is easily preventable.

Without a cure, we pushed on with living, with making the most of every day, with meds and therapy, and with prayers raised from the Basilica of Baltimore to the Grotto of Lourdes. Together we learned how to master movement with doggie carts supporting her rear legs. The day she came through her neurologist's clinic door in her cart, the entire staff came into the lobby and cheered with smiles and tears as they watched her proudly roll forward to the treatment room under her own power.

Pecos became an ambassador for BROOD, attending doggie events and participating in fundraising walks. She alternated between her doggie cart and her Red Flyer wagon, which was known as her chariot. People applauded her effort to walk and asked to have their pictures taken with her. She adored the attention and gave a kiss to anyone who wanted one. She had a special fondness for licking the feet of squealing, excited babies.

Five months into our journey, Pecos lost the use of her front legs. Still happy with Hoover's companionship, good food, and her pile of quilts with a view to outdoor activity and TV shows, we were now in hospice mode. At least Pecos was pain free and reveling in outings with the Red Flyer wagon.

One month later Pecos let me know it was time to let her go. I gave her a final ride in the Red Flyer wagon, embraced her with our love, and then helped her on a peaceful transition from wheels to wings.

Pecos may be one of the few dogs in rescue history to be adopted after her passing. Some may think it a moot point; she was in foster care and considered unadoptable because of her terminal prognosis. But it did not seem quite right to close the books without making it official. She was part of our family. She was treasured. She was loved. To this day I think of her with that infamous question put forth by many a foster parent: "Who rescued whom?" She was so amazing.

 *Diane McManus*

We adopted our first Basset Hound when my husband and I were engaged. Bogart was eight months old with a genetic illness called panosteitis that caused him to have periodic lameness for the first few months. He responded positively to treatment and recovered completely. I have always loved Basset Hounds, but as I look back now at the last 12 years, I realize I knew very little about them at that time. With love and patience, Bogart has taught me everything I need to know, which I want to share with any future Basset Hound moms and dads, so you can be better educated.

First, buy a king-sized mattress before you bring a Hound into your home. Despite what Daddy says, this hound will sleep at your feet, next to your body, or horizontal in the middle of the bed, regardless of how many doggie beds you make available. It's better if you just give in to this fact now and focus on finding a small corner of the bed where you can sleep.

Second, don't leave a Basset puppy alone when there is any possibility of fireworks. I had no idea we could hear fireworks where we lived. We went to a friend's house one night, and I specifically left Bogart home, as I thought he would be safer. I came home to a winter wonderland of couch stuffing that had snowed all over the living room!

Third, never have children without a Hound. Hounds are good at staying with the baby until they fall asleep, and then coming to find you when they wake up. They can kiss wounds to make them feel better, and they are the experts at waking a sleeping child for school with kisses, resulting in a far better attitude than if Mom had woken said child.

Fourth, nurse your baby with one hand and pet your Basset with the other. Why not, when there is a perfectly good half of your lap wide open? Any respectable Hound will be sure not to waste of this opportunity.

Fifth, if you want the best seat in the house, you need to move the Basset Hound. I saw this on a pillow once and thought that it must have been created by someone who visited my house. We traded in a standard three-seat sofa for a large, angled sofa with recliners specifically because I got tired of watching movies on the floor while the kids and dogs were on the couch.

Sixth, there is no tragedy or stress so terrible that a long cuddle with your Basset can't make better. Seriously, as far as anti-anxiety medicine goes, cuddling with Bogart is extremely effective, with no side effects.

Lastly, help your Hound to age with grace and dignity. Bogart has a laundry list of medical issues, many of which have spanned more than half his life and taken a huge portion of the checking account. However, through it all, he greets each day with a kiss on my cheek and a wag of his tail. He will happily go anywhere I am going and still loves go for walks at age 13.

Over his lifetime, Bogart has seen my husband and me get married and bring home two beautiful baby boys, helped me through two miscarriages, moved with us into two different houses, vacationed at grandma's, welcomed two Labrador Retrievers into our home, cried with me when I had to send one to the Rainbow Bridge, and mentored several foster Basset Hounds for the Arizona Basset Hound Rescue.

I hope I can live up to his standards and be half the friend he has been to me. I know that soon his day to go the Rainbow Bridge will come. I write this in tribute to the one companion that has taught me more than I could ever put into print, loved me more than I ever deserved, and inspired me to further help Hounds like him to make differences in people's lives.

I love you, sweet Bogart, more than tears and words could ever do justice.

 *Sharon Novy*

What Being Owned by Basset Hounds Means to Me:

☑ I never have to use an alarm clock (they will let me know it's breakfast time).

☑ I have a friend and loyal companion *fur*ever.

☑ My doorbell has automatic barking when someone arrives at the house.

☑ I have unlimited dog hair to clean up (yay!).

- ☑ There's always drool on my favorite outfits.

- ☑ Arriving home means receiving a great happy dance.

- ☑ Arriving home means an enthusiastic retelling of my Hounds' day via howling.

- ☑ I can never forget my daily exercise.

- ☑ There's always a warm body to spoon with as I sleep.

- ☑ I am awakened ever so gently with a Basset nose in my face and a wagging tail.

- ☑ I'll never forget supper time; it's five o'clock somewhere!

- ☑ I can't miss taking time out from my hectic day to give belly rubs, play with favorite toys, or play chase around the house or yard.

- ☑ I get unconditional love for a lifetime!

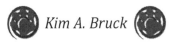 *Kim A. Bruck*

About Happy Tails Books™

Happy Tails Books™ was created to help support animal rescue efforts by showcasing the love and joy adopted dogs have to offer. With the help of animal rescue groups, stories are submitted by people who have adopted dogs, and then Happy Tails Books™ compiles them into breed-specific books. These books serve not only to entertain but also to educate readers about dog adoption and the characteristics of each specific type of dog. Happy Tails Books™ donates a significant portion of proceeds back to the rescue groups that help gather stories for the books.

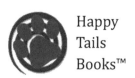 Happy Tails Books™

To submit a story or learn about other books Happy Tails Books™ publishes, please visit our website at http://happytailsbooks.com.

49502860R00081

Made in the USA
Lexington, KY
08 February 2016